1314
AND ALL THAT

SCOULAR ANDERSON

1314
AND ALL THAT

SCOULAR ANDERSON

BIRLINN

for Jennifer

First published in Great Britain in 2000 by
Birlinn Limited
West Newington House
10 Newington Road
Edinburgh EH9 1QS

www.birlinn.co.uk

Reprinted 2005, 2011

First published by
Canongate Books Ltd
14 High Street
Edinburgh EH1 1TH

ISBN13: 978 1 84158 051 7

British Library Cataloguing-in-Publication Data
A Catalogue record for this book is available from
the British Library

Printed and bound by CPI Antony Rowe, Chippenham and Eastbourne

CONTENTS

SCOTLAND GETS ITS ACT TOGETHER: THE END OF THE ICE AGE

10,000 YEARS	9,000	8,000	7,000	6,000	5,000	4,000	3,000	2,000	1,000 BC	AD	1,000	2,000

ICE DEPARTS   YOU ARE HERE

Around 10,000 BC the ice which covered Scotland began to melt. Heavy ice is not good for your skin. Result: Scotland had a bad complexion – rock, slime, sludge, scratches, mud and more mud.

However, help was at hand. As the ice retreated northwards, life moved up from the south. After a 2,000-year-long facial, Scotland didn't look too bad. There were grasses, mosses, bushes and trees. By 8,000 BC there were birch trees growing in the north of Scotland. Then came insects, birds and animals.

SCOTLAND UNDER HERE

AT THIS TIME THE BIT OF LAND WE CALL BRITAIN WAS STILL CONNECTED TO THE BIT OF LAND WE CALL EUROPE. THERE WAS NO ENGLISH CHANNEL.

CROSS HERE

THE ARRIVAL of PEOPLE   The STONE AGE AND THE NEW STONE AGE

10,000 YEARS	9,000	8,000	7,000	6,000	5,000	4,000	3,000	2,000	1,000	BC AD	1,000	2,000

PEOPLE ARRIVE   FARMERS ARRIVE

After the animals came the people – not many of them. They didn't stay in one place very long, as their meals kept moving – animals had to be chased and berries had to be searched for.

The hunters and their families lived near the coasts in temporary tents. A stake or two holding up skins, branches and rushes was fine for them.

THESE PEOPLE SET UP BASE IN SCOTLAND AROUND 6,000 YEARS BC. THEY ARE KNOWN AS STONE AGE PEOPLE BECAUSE MANY OF THE TOOLS AND WEAPONS THEY USED WERE CARVED OUT OF STONE.

THE LIVES OF THE PEOPLE WERE SHORT AND HARD. MANY OF THE ANIMALS THEY HUNTED WERE DANGEROUS. THEY MADE TRAPS FOR ANIMALS AND FISH OR HUNTED THEM WITH SPEARS OR HARPOONS TIPPED WITH BONE BARBS.

THINGS THEY MADE FROM STONE, BONE OR ANTLERS INCLUDED KNIVES, PINS, SCRAPERS, ARROW-HEADS AND HOLE-BORERS.

Hey, let's make do with hedgehog sandwich!

8

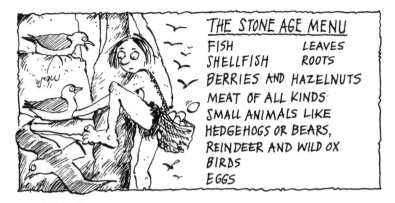

THE STONE AGE MENU
FISH   LEAVES
SHELLFISH   ROOTS
BERRIES AND HAZELNUTS
MEAT OF ALL KINDS
SMALL ANIMALS LIKE
HEDGEHOGS OR BEARS,
REINDEER AND WILD OX
BIRDS
EGGS

Melting ice produces water – lots of it. Soon, sea-levels began to rise and the bit of land we call Britain was cut off from the rest of Europe. That didn't stop a brave prehistoric tourist in a boat. Scotland was a mountainous, boggy place full of forests. It was easier to travel by sea than by land and so the people kept coming.

OLD MODEL BOAT CARVED OUT OF TREE TRUNK

NEW MODEL BOAT MADE OF SKINS STRETCHED OVER FRAMEWORK OF BRANCHES

9

Around 4,000 BC the latest people to arrive in Scotland brought a brilliant idea: Instead of chasing animals for food, keep them nearby. Saves a lot of time. These farmers brought herds of sheep, cattle, pigs, goats, and grain to sow. They chopped down trees to make spaces for growing crops. They had digging sticks, wooden hoes, and axes of polished stone.

THE AXE WAS AN IMPORTANT PIECE OF STONE AGE EQUIPMENT. AXE HEADS MADE OF STONE FROM IRELAND AND THE NORTH OF ENGLAND HAVE BEEN FOUND IN SCOTLAND. PERHAPS THE FARMERS IN SCOTLAND EXCHANGED SOMETHING — A BEARSKIN, FOR INSTANCE - FOR A GOOD AXE. THIS WOULD HAVE BEEN THE BEGINNINGS OF TRADE.

This is the latest, deluxe model - notice the great handling and balance!

These people lived in what is called the New Stone Age. Compared to the Old Stone Age, life could now be considered very modern.

Clothes were made of fur and animal skins. The people decorated themselves with jewellery of bones and shells.

Because the early farmers didn't need to go hunting every day they could stay in one place, which gave them time to improve their architecture and interior design. They built houses with walls of wood and turf, roofs of rushes and heather. They built houses of stone, too, and some have survived.

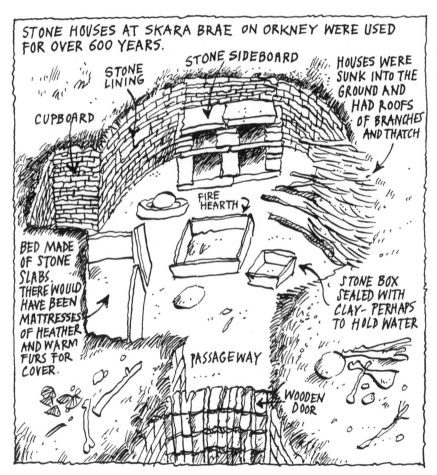

STONE HOUSES AT SKARA BRAE ON ORKNEY WERE USED FOR OVER 600 YEARS.

STONE SIDEBOARD

STONE LINING

HOUSES WERE SUNK INTO THE GROUND AND HAD ROOFS OF BRANCHES AND THATCH

CUPBOARD

FIRE HEARTH

BED MADE OF STONE SLABS. THERE WOULD HAVE BEEN MATTRESSES OF HEATHER AND WARM FURS FOR COVER.

STONE BOX SEALED WITH CLAY- PERHAPS TO HOLD WATER

PASSAGEWAY

WOODEN DOOR

The Stone Age farmers built stone houses for the dead, too. The dead were buried in underground chambers lined with stone slabs and covered with a mound of earth or a cairn. Very impressive but dark, crowded and smelly – especially when filled with a hundred years of dead relatives.

MAES HOWE BURIAL CHAMBER ON ORKNEY WAS BUILT SKILFULLY OF STONE SLABS. THE WALLS SLOPE INWARDS TO FORM THE ROOF. THERE ARE STONE BUTTRESSES (PILLARS) AT EACH CORNER TO STRENGTHEN THE BUILDING. THE DEAD WERE BURIED IN SMALL CHAMBERS IN THE WALLS OF THE MAIN ROOM.

OUTSIDE VIEW OF MAES HOWE. THE PASSAGE INTO THE CHAMBER IS 16m LONG. ON THE SHORTEST DAY OF THE YEAR THE SUN SHINES DIRECTLY INTO THE DOORWAY.

DITCH

When the people became settled in their farmsteads and food was plentiful and life wasn't so harsh, they discovered something -- free time. And what did they do with it? They started to get big ideas. They built circles and rows of giant stones. Now this sort of thing needed planning and organization. It needed teamwork and a leader. Someone was getting bossy. These people were dividing themselves into tribes with chiefs.

It would have been helpful if these people had left a note explaining what exactly these stone monuments were for, but as they hadn't got the hang of writing, the stones remain a bit of a mystery.

THE STONE AGE PEOPLE CARVED BEAUTIFUL PATTERNS ON STONE. SPIRALS AND 'CUP-AND-RING' SHAPES WERE A FAVOURITE DESIGN.

THEY CARVED HARD LUMPS OF VOLCANIC ROCK INTO STRANGE OBJECTS. IT'S NOT CLEAR WHAT THESE WERE USED FOR. THEY MAY HAVE BEEN SYMBOLS OF POWER.

This will give them something to think about in a few thousand years' time!

Now answer this: Is a bendy sword enough protection? Do you think you might also need: a) a ditch, b) some water, c) a high wall, d) a palisade, e) all of these?

THE DISCOVERY OF METAL — THE BRONZE AGE AND THE IRON AGE

| 10,000 YEARS | 9,000 | 8,000 | 7,000 | 6,000 | 5,000 | 4,000 | 3,000 | 2,000 | 1,000 | BC | AD | 1,000 | 2,000 |

BRONZE IN USE ABOUT → ← IRON IN USE

Around 1,800 BC more new people arrived. They had the idea that the dead travelled on to another world; so when a relative died he or she was tucked into a stone slab box along with a clay pot of food (a snack for the journey) and some of his or her favourite things (jewellery or arrowheads). But hang on a moment – these things are made of metal. Time to throw away that stone axe and get one made of copper or bronze – they're the latest thing!

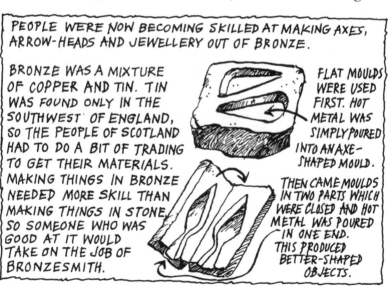

PEOPLE WERE NOW BECOMING SKILLED AT MAKING AXES, ARROW-HEADS AND JEWELLERY OUT OF BRONZE.

BRONZE WAS A MIXTURE OF COPPER AND TIN. TIN WAS FOUND ONLY IN THE SOUTHWEST OF ENGLAND, SO THE PEOPLE OF SCOTLAND HAD TO DO A BIT OF TRADING TO GET THEIR MATERIALS. MAKING THINGS IN BRONZE NEEDED MORE SKILL THAN MAKING THINGS IN STONE, SO SOMEONE WHO WAS GOOD AT IT WOULD TAKE ON THE JOB OF BRONZESMITH.

FLAT MOULDS WERE USED FIRST. HOT METAL WAS SIMPLY POURED INTO AN AXE-SHAPED MOULD.

THEN CAME MOULDS IN TWO PARTS WHICH WERE CLOSED AND HOT METAL WAS POURED IN ONE END. THIS PRODUCED BETTER-SHAPED OBJECTS.

Life in the Bronze Age was fairly comfortable, for a while ...

OXEN USED TO PULL PLOUGH

FIELDS DIVIDED BY WALLS OR FENCES

HUTS IN GROUPS MADE OF TURF, STONES OR WATTLE AND DAUB (WOVEN TWIGS COVERED IN MUD)

BARLEY GROUND INTO FLOUR

... until there seemed to be an awful lot of people about. Farmland was getting scarce. If you couldn't set up farm yourself, you'd have to work for someone else. A change in climate led to rain and cold which led to crop failure which led to empty stomachs. Time to grab some extra land from your neighbour. Time to invent the *sword* ...

Let's face it, the sword wasn't invented for shaving with. It had only two uses:

a) threatening to kill people

b) killing people.

ABOUT 700 BC PEOPLE BEGAN USING A NEW METAL CALLED IRON. IT WAS MUCH HARDER THAN BRONZE AND WAS EASIER TO TURN INTO USEFUL OBJECTS.

IRON HAD TO BE 'TEMPERED' (HEATED AND COOLED) TO MAKE IT HARD AND STRONG.

SOME OF THE FIRST SWORD-USERS DIDN'T GET THE HANG OF THAT, SO THEY HAD TO STOP FIGHTING NOW AND THEN TO STRAIGHTEN THEIR WEAPONS.

Hang on a mo'!

People were getting anxious about aggression. At any moment a neighbouring tribe might appear brandishing their swords, so it was wise to make it difficult for dangerous visitors. Surrounding your village with a deep ditch and earth rampart helped. Better still if there was a high fence and a strong gate, too.

Sometimes villages were built on top of hills. This allowed the inhabitants to see people coming, but living on top of a hill wasn't very convenient.

DESIRABLE SECOND HOME: THE BROCH.
WHEN STRANGE PEOPLE ARE SEEN IN YOUR AREA CARRYING SWORDS OR SPEARS, RETREAT INTO THIS COMFORTABLE TOWER. ALL MOD. CONS. ONLY AVAILABLE IN AREAS WITH SUITABLE, FLAT BUILDING STONE. NO WINDOWS AND A SMALL DOOR MEAN EXTRA SECURITY. PARAPET AT TOP CAN BE USED FOR FLINGING TAUNTS AT ENEMY.

Iron Age life could still be enjoyable. While a man was away dealing with the neighbours from hell, his wife could prepare a meal flavoured with herbs, throw on a nice little dress woven from cloth, decorate herself with fine jewellery and pour out some beer made from barley for his return.

If you found your way blocked by a large ditch and a long mound of earth, would you assume it had been made by: a) an earthquake, b) a giant mole, c) Romans?

BC	AD	100	200	300	400	500	600	700	800	900	1000	1100	1200	1300	1400	1500	1600	1700	1800	1900	2000

0 ● COMING ● GOING

Rome began as a city in 753 BC and grew into a huge empire that lasted about 800 years. The Romans just kept adding bits on until the empire stretched from the Atlantic Ocean to the Middle East. The Romans always gave reasons for their conquests:

FIVE GOOD REASONS WHY WE SHOULD TAKE OVER YOUR TERRITORY:

I   WE DO THINGS WELL. YOU'LL LIKE OUR SYSTEM.

II YOU'VE GOT SOMETHING WE NEED (E.G. - A USEFUL MINERAL).

III IT IMPRESSES FOLK BACK HOME.

IV AS NEIGHBOURS YOU'RE BECOMING A TEENSY-WEENSY BIT OF A NUISANCE.

V   WE'RE GOING TO DO IT ANYWAY, JUST FOR THE HELL OF IT.

What's this?

Search me!

23

It may well have been that a new Roman emperor called Claudius wanted to create a bit of a splash. In AD 43 he ordered part of his army to cross the Channel and invade England.

To celebrate my crowning as emperor, I want you to conquer all that bit.

By AD 80 the Roman army had reached Scotland, led by their general Gnaeus Julius Agricola. Of course, Scotland wasn't called Scotland at that time. It was just a piece of land where many different tribes lived.

The Romans usually tried to get tribes to submit peacefully. Often a bribe did the trick. If the locals got awkward, the army was sent in. If the locals kept on being awkward, the Romans turned nasty. It seems that the tribes in the south of Scotland were a push-over so, General Agricola marched on and soon reached the narrow middle of Scotland between the River Clyde and the River Forth.

AGRICOLA HAD ALREADY SENT HIS SHIPS ROUND SCOTLAND, SO HE KNEW HOW MUCH THERE WAS TO CONQUER.

WILD, MOUNTAINOUS BITS

SHIPS WITH SUPPLIES

ROMAN FORTS

BOGGY BIT

RIVER FORTH

BORDER (TODAY)

RIVER CLYDE

ROMANS

AT THAT TIME THE LANDSCAPE LOOKED DIFFERENT FROM NOW. THE RIVER FORTH WAS WIDER AND STRETCHED FURTHER INLAND. ALSO, WHERE THE RIVER NARROWED, THE LAND WAS VERY BOGGY AND WET SO THE NORTHERN PART OF SCOTLAND LOOKED ALMOST LIKE ANOTHER ISLAND. SOME OF THE LOCALS WOULD HAVE BEEN WILLING TO ACT AS GUIDES OR SPIES — FOR THE RIGHT PRICE.

Psst!

Want some info?

25

The tribes in the north were not so willing to submit to the Romans. After a lot of skirmishing the two sides lined up for a proper battle. It was fought at what the Romans called Mons Graupius, somewhere in the north-east.

The local tribes were called the Caledonii and were led by their chief, Calgacus. He is the first person in Scottish history whose name we know. Before the battle he made a stirring speech to his men.

The Romans create a desert and they call it peace!

THE CALEDONII HAD LONG SWORDS, SMALL SHIELDS AND NO ARMOUR. THEY ALSO USED CHARIOTS WHICH WERE NOT VERY EFFICIENT AND ALREADY RATHER OLD-FASHIONED.

The locals didn't stand a chance against the well-disciplined Roman army ...

THE TALLY OF THE DEAD MONS GRAUPIUS CALEDONII – 10,000 ROMANS – 360*	*ACCORDING TO THE ROMANS, ANYWAY

After the victory, Agricola's tour of duty was finished, so he packed his bags and went home.

For the next three hundred years the Romans couldn't decide what to do in Scotland. They got so fed up with the troublesome Scottish tribes they decided a high wall would stop the hassle. It was built of stone, tall and wide, and it stretched from coast to coast across the north of England just south of the present border.

Twenty years later, the Romans decided to move closer to the trouble spots, so another, smaller wall was built between the River Clyde and the River Forth. It was only three metres high, built of turf on a stone base.

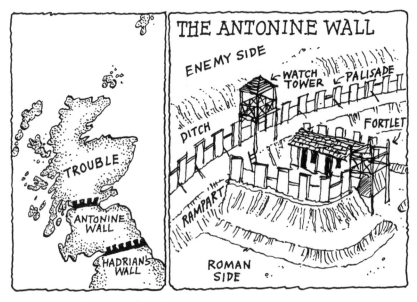

The Romans couldn't make up their minds about the walls. They kept abandoning them, then rebuilding and reoccupying them. But Roman eyes were everywhere. The countryside was dotted with forts connected with good roads.

THE ROMAN ARMY WAS DIVIDED INTO LEGIONS
(OF ABOUT 5,000 MEN) AND AUXILIARIES (HELPERS –
WHICH INCLUDED SOLDIERS ON HORSEBACK – THE CAVALRY).
SOME SOLDIERS HAD SPECIAL JOBS – LIKE CARPENTERS,
CLERKS, ACCOUNTANTS, DOCTORS, ARMOURERS, ARCHITECTS ETC.

BESIDES WEAPONS (SWORDS, SPEARS, JAVELINS) AND SHIELD,
EACH SOLDIER HAD TO CARRY EXTRA CLOTHES,
FOOD RATIONS,
COOKING POTS
AND TOOLS
LIKE AXES,
SAWS,
PICKS,
SPADES
AND
TURF-
CUTTERS.

WHEN
NOT IN
USE, THEIR
SHIELDS
WERE
COVERED
WITH A
PIECE OF
LEATHER
TO PROTECT
THE PAINTWORK.

THE ARMY WAS ACCOMPANIED ON THE MARCH BY
COUNTLESS WAGONS PULLED BY MULES OR OXEN. THE WAGONS
CARRIED BULKY ITEMS LIKE TENTS, COOKING EQUIPMENT,
BARRELS, AND FODDER FOR THE ANIMALS.

FEW OF THE SOLDIERS WOULD HAVE BEEN ROMANS.
MEN WERE RECRUITED FROM ALL CORNERS OF THE EMPIRE,
PERHAPS SPAIN, GERMANY OR BULGARIA. MANY YOUNG MEN
FROM TRIBES IN SCOTLAND WOULD HAVE JOINED UP AND
BEEN SENT OFF TO SERVE IN THE ARMY IN A DISTANT COUNTRY.

29

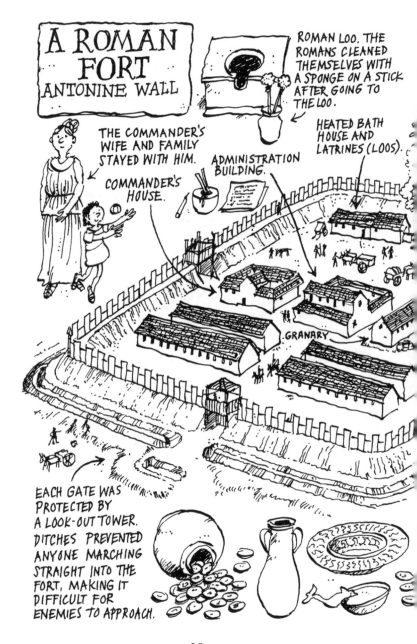

A ROMAN FORT
ANTONINE WALL

ROMAN LOO. THE ROMANS CLEANED THEMSELVES WITH A SPONGE ON A STICK AFTER GOING TO THE LOO.

THE COMMANDER'S WIFE AND FAMILY STAYED WITH HIM.

COMMANDER'S HOUSE.

ADMINISTRATION BUILDING.

HEATED BATH HOUSE AND LATRINES (LOOS).

GRANARY

EACH GATE WAS PROTECTED BY A LOOK-OUT TOWER. DITCHES PREVENTED ANYONE MARCHING STRAIGHT INTO THE FORT, MAKING IT DIFFICULT FOR ENEMIES TO APPROACH.

30

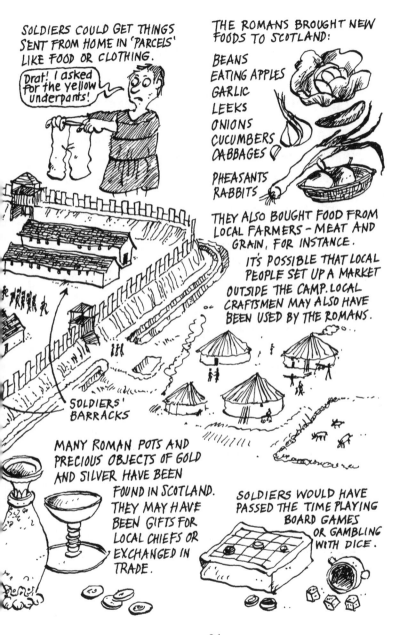

SOLDIERS COULD GET THINGS SENT FROM HOME IN 'PARCELS' LIKE FOOD OR CLOTHING.

Drat! I asked for the yellow underpants!

THE ROMANS BROUGHT NEW FOODS TO SCOTLAND:

BEANS
EATING APPLES
GARLIC
LEEKS
ONIONS
CUCUMBERS
CABBAGES

PHEASANTS
RABBITS

THEY ALSO BOUGHT FOOD FROM LOCAL FARMERS – MEAT AND GRAIN, FOR INSTANCE.

IT'S POSSIBLE THAT LOCAL PEOPLE SET UP A MARKET OUTSIDE THE CAMP. LOCAL CRAFTSMEN MAY ALSO HAVE BEEN USED BY THE ROMANS.

SOLDIERS' BARRACKS

MANY ROMAN POTS AND PRECIOUS OBJECTS OF GOLD AND SILVER HAVE BEEN FOUND IN SCOTLAND. THEY MAY HAVE BEEN GIFTS FOR LOCAL CHIEFS OR EXCHANGED IN TRADE.

SOLDIERS WOULD HAVE PASSED THE TIME PLAYING BOARD GAMES OR GAMBLING WITH DICE.

31

Scotland never really became part of the Roman Empire. There could have been various reasons for this:

REASONS WHY WE'RE LEAVING

I   YOUR LOCAL TRIBES ARE TOO FEROCIOUS AND TOO MUCH OF A NUISANCE.

II   YOUR COUNTRY IS TOO WILD AND BARREN TO BE OF ANY USE.

III IT'S DIFFICULT TO CONTROL THE MOUNTAINS AND THE GLENS.

IV   IT'S TOO FAR AWAY FROM HQ IN ROME.

V   OUR EMPIRE IS FALLING APART AT THE SEAMS ANYWAY.

GOODBYE   The Romans

About AD 380 the Romans left for good. They destroyed their forts and the contents so that the locals wouldn't benefit from them. The Romans soon became a distant memory.

So you thought an Angle was a corner and a Pict was used for digging holes? Just to confuse things: Why were the Scots Irish and the Britons speaking Welsh?

SCOTLAND STILL IN BITS THE FOUR PEOPLES

BC	AD																			
0	100	200	300	400	500	600	700	800	900	1000	1100	1200	1300	1400	1500	1600	1700	1800	1900	2000

PICTS, SCOTS, ETC. →

When the Romans arrived there were lots of tribes living in Scotland. They attacked one another as much as they attacked the Romans. Big, pushy tribes won, of course, and by the time the Romans left, the land was divided between four peoples.

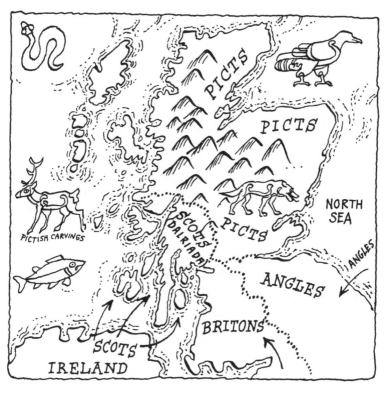

33

So this is how things stood: The Scots, who were Irish (confused?), came and settled on the west coast, nearest their homeland. They called the new kingdom Dalriada, and their king lived in a fort on the rock of Dunadd. (Today this area is called Argyll.)

The Britons lived in the south-west, mostly in the Clyde valley. Their kingdom was called Strathclyde, and the king lived in a fortress on a rock.

They called the rock Alcluth but others called it Dun Briton – the Fort of the Britons (nowadays known as Dumbarton).

The Britons had been driven north by the Angles and Saxons. They had come across the North Sea to settle in south-east Scotland. Their kingdom stretched southwards from the River Forth into the land which was soon to be called Angle Land (or England).

The Picts lived in the north. It was others who gave them the name Picts, perhaps meaning 'painted', because of their habit of decorating their bodies with dyes or tattoos.

EACH OF THESE PEOPLES NOW HAD A KING. THE KING MOVED AROUND HIS KINGDOM SO HE COULD BE SEEN BY HIS SUBJECTS OR CLAN. HE WOULD ALSO COLLECT TRIBUTES – FOOD, CATTLE, OR PERHAPS THE OFFER OF WORK OR MILITARY SERVICE. THE KING WOULD HAVE BEEN ACCOMPANIED BY HIS RETINUE– BODYGUARDS, ADVISERS, PRIESTS, A SOOTHSAYER RESPONSIBLE FOR THE LAWS, AND A POET WHO MEMORIZED HEROIC DEEDS OR FAMILY HISTORY (NOTHING WAS WRITTEN DOWN).

The peoples of Scotland didn't live happily together. There were plenty of career opportunities for skilful warriors.

Society was now becoming pyramid-shaped. If you were one of the many at the bottom of the heap, you would spend your life working hard on the land. If you were one of the lucky few near to the king, life was a bit more pleasurable, with time for leisure activities like hunting and hawking.

The Men with the Message are here. You may be asked to stand outside with a sprig of mistletoe or inside with a cross. What's your choice?

ANOTHER ARRIVAL CHRISTIANITY

BC	AD																				
0	100	200	300	400	500	600	700	800	900	1000	1100	1200	1300	1400	1500	1600	1700	1800	1900	2000

CHRISTIANITY ARRIVES   COLUMBA ARRIVES

At this time people worshipped many kinds of gods – ones that lived in trees or mountains or animals. People dropped precious things like swords or jewellery into lochs and rivers. They hoped these gifts would please the spirits that lived there and would bring good luck.

I need five dogs...   ...and a small rat.

There were priests called Druids. They were fresh-air types who held mysterious ceremonies in the middle of woods. They killed animals – and sometimes humans – as sacrifices to the gods.

During Roman times a new religion spread from the east – Christianity. Not much is known about the first men with the Christian message, but we know some of their names – like Mungo and Ninian. Nowadays the word saint (meaning holy) is added to their names.

We know more about one called Columba. He belonged to a noble Irish family, bore battle scars and did something to offend his people, because in AD 563 he was banished from Ireland. He sailed to

38

Scotland with twelve others and set up a monastery on the island of Iona. Columba then went off to talk to the mainland about Christianity.

Not everyone was keen to become a Christian, so the old and new religions existed side by side for a long time.

COLUMBA AND HIS COMPANIONS WOULD HAVE BEEN CRAFTSMEN AND FARMERS, AS THEY HAD TO BUILD THEIR OWN CHURCH AND HOMES AND PRODUCE THEIR OWN FOOD. COLUMBA'S MONASTERY ON IONA MIGHT HAVE LOOKED SOMETHING LIKE THIS.

Will it be bad when Thorfinn comes visiting? Will it be worse when he brings his granny? Will he send a postcard first?

YET MORE ARRIVALS THE VIKINGS

BC	AD																			
0	100	200	300	400	500	600	700	800	900	1000	1100	1200	1300	1400	1500	1600	1700	1800	1900	2000

VIKING TROUBLE

It was a terrifying day when Thorfinn Thicknose arrived. It was even more terrifying when he brought his family.

Hi, there!

We're your new neighbours!

A Viking diary might have looked something like this:

WINTER: SIT AROUND FIRE, DRINKS, SAGAS, SONGS, MORE DRINKS.

SPRING: RAIDING AND TRADING.

SUMMER: FARMING.

AUTUMN: MORE RAIDING AND TRADING. OUR NEW SHIP.

MEMO: SEEN A NICE LITTLE BIT OF LAND IN SCOTLAND THAT WOULD DO FOR MY RETIREMENT.

40

The Vikings were smooth operators. They raided for silverware, cattle, slaves. Then they travelled across Europe to trade these goods for luxury items. Their slim, narrow longships took them anywhere.

When farmland became scarce back home in Norway, the Vikings began to settle in other places. The north of Scotland and most of the islands became Viking territory. As a result, lots of places gained Viking names.

Which early Scottish king said: 'I could have done so much but I just didn't find the time'?

In 843 two of the kingdoms of Scotland joined together and became one. Kenneth MacAlpin, King of the Scots in Dalriada, became King of the Picts as well. It seems to have been a peaceful arrangement, perhaps because his mother was a Pictish princess.

The new kingdom was known as Alba and although the new king is known as Kenneth I, first King of Scots, the country was still divided into three parts.

Kenneth moved the capital of his kingdom from Dunadd to Scone. He was proclaimed king while sitting on a special stone, now known as the *Stone of Destiny* or *Stone of Scone*.

When Kenneth died, the kingdom didn't pass to his son but to his brother. The early Scottish kings used a system called *Tanistry* to choose a new king. During the lifetime of a king, the next king would be chosen. He was called *Tanaiste Rig* – 'the Second to the King'.

IF THE JOB OF KING PASSED FROM FATHER TO SON AND IF THE KING DIED TOO SOON, THE NEW KING MIGHT STILL ONLY BE A BOY — TRICKY SITUATION.

AT LEAST WITH TANISTRY YOU COULD CHOOSE SOMEONE WHO WAS THE RIGHT AGE TO BE NEXT KING.

ON THE OTHER HAND...

ONCE THE TANAISTE RIG HAD BEEN CHOSEN HE MIGHT WELL GET FED UP WAITING FOR THE KING TO DIE NATURALLY...

The first kings of Scotland (known as the House of Alpin) were a disorganized lot. When they weren't fighting off the Vikings they were killing each other. Not many of these kings died peacefully in their beds.

43

DONALD I
REIGNED 4 YEARS
859-863
KENNETH MACALPIN'S
BROTHER

PROBABLY MURDERED.

CONSTANTINE I
REIGNED 14 YEARS
863-877
KENNETH'S ELDER
SON

SPENT HIS REIGN
FENDING OFF VIKINGS.
KILLED BY A GROUP
OF VIKINGS CALLED
THE DARK STRANGERS.

AED
REIGNED 1 YEAR
877-878
KENNETH'S YOUNGER
SON

MURDERED BY HIS
COUSIN GIRIC.

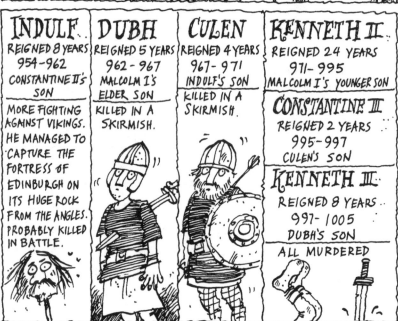

INDULF
REIGNED 8 YEARS
954-962
CONSTANTINE II's
SON

MORE FIGHTING
AGAINST VIKINGS.
HE MANAGED TO
CAPTURE THE
FORTRESS OF
EDINBURGH ON
ITS HUGE ROCK
FROM THE ANGLES.
PROBABLY KILLED
IN BATTLE.

DUBH
REIGNED 5 YEARS
962-967
MALCOLM I's
ELDER SON

KILLED IN A
SKIRMISH.

CULEN
REIGNED 4 YEARS
967-971
INDULF'S SON

KILLED IN A
SKIRMISH.

KENNETH II
REIGNED 24 YEARS
971-995
MALCOLM I'S YOUNGER SON

CONSTANTINE III
REIGNED 2 YEARS
995-997
CULEN'S SON

KENNETH III
REIGNED 8 YEARS
997-1005
DUBH'S SON

ALL MURDERED

44

EOCHAN AND GIRIC	DONALD II	CONSTANTINE II	MALCOLM I
REIGNED 11 YEARS 878-889 AED'S NEPHEW AND DONALD'S SON	REIGNED 11 YEARS 889-900 CONSTANTINE'S SON	REIGNED 43 YEARS 900-943 *WELL DONE!* AED'S SON	REIGNED 11 YEARS 943-954 DONALD II'S SON
STRANGE DOUBLE-KING ARRANGEMENT. BOTH PROBABLY MURDERED.	SPENT HIS REIGN FIGHTING VIKINGS WHO TOOK OVER NORTH OF ENGLAND. SCOTLAND NOW SURROUNDED BY VIKINGS. PROBABLY POISONED.	MORE FIGHTING WITH VIKINGS AND ANGLES. BEST OF A BAD BUNCH. RETIRED TO A MONASTERY AT ST. ANDREWS.	AGREED TO HELP ANGLES AGAINST VIKINGS. ATTACKED ANGLES INSTEAD. KILLED IN BATTLE.

HANDY THINGS TO DO WITH YOUR ENEMY'S HEAD.

IT WAS THE CUSTOM IN THESE TIMES TO CUT OFF YOUR ENEMY'S HEAD BECAUSE IT WOULD BRING LUCK IN FUTURE BATTLES. THE HEAD WAS SOMETIMES STUCK ON A POLE OUTSIDE THE VICTOR'S HOUSE OR TIED TO A SPEAR. A VIKING CALLED SIGURA ONCE TIED A HEAD TO HIS SADDLE BUT AS HE RODE, A TOOTH PUNCTURED SIGURA'S LEG AND HE LATER DIED OF BLOOD POISONING.

Will the Scots give the Angles anguish? Will the Mormaers give the Scots stress? Did Duncan have all the right connections?

BC	AD																				
0	100	200	300	400	500	600	700	800	900	1000	1100	1200	1300	1400	1500	1600	1700	1800	1900	2000	

BATTLE OF CARHAM

During the reign of King Malcolm II two things happened which made the Scots feel big.

Though the Angles lived in the land south of the River Forth, the Scots claimed it was really theirs. In 1018 Malcolm decided to sort the matter out once and for all. He marched to the River Tweed, defeated the Angles at the Battle of Carham and, hey presto, the kingdom of Scots was a bit bigger.

Then there was another spot of luck. Owen the Bald, King of the Britons, died. Who was the nearest relative who could claim his job? A man called Duncan – who just happened to be Malcolm's grandson. And when Malcolm died, who was his heir? Well ... Duncan ... who found himself king of a Scotland, which now looked much as it does today.

THE KINGS OF SCOTLAND NOW LIKED TO THINK THEY RULED OVER THE WHOLE COUNTRY. NOT SO. THERE WERE STILL BITS THEY DIDN'T CONTROL. BIT NUMBER ONE: THE NORTHERN MAINLAND AND THE WESTERN AND NORTHERN ISLES – STILL OCCUPIED BY VIKINGS.

BIT NUMBER TWO: LARGE CHUNK OF THE HIGHLANDS. THIS WAS CONTROLLED BY THE MORMAERS (EARLS) OF MORAY WHO WERE BAD NEWS FOR SCOTTISH KINGS.

Never trust a Mormaer!

ATLANTIC OCEAN

ORKNEY

SHETLAND

WESTERN ISLES

VIKINGS

VIKINGS

VIKINGS

VIKINGS

MORMAERS

SCOTLAND

VIKINGS

RIVER FORTH

NORTH SEA

EDINBURGH

MALCOLM ADDS THIS BIT

CARHAM

RIVER TWEED

DUNCAN GETS THIS BIT

ANGLES

We'll be back!

Huh!

IRELAND

Why should you never say: 'Cowardie Custard!' to The Conqueror? 'Torn tights!' to Queen Margaret? 'Get on your boat!' to a Viking?

KING DUNCAN I TO KING EDGAR.

Like all Scottish kings so far, Duncan liked a good fight. The trouble was that battles had a habit of shortening your life. Duncan had only ruled for six years when he picked a fight with Macbeth, Mormaer of Moray. (Never trust a Mormaer!) Macbeth killed Duncan and became the new king of Scots.

Macbeth seems to have been quite a good king (though Shakespeare made up some nasty things about him centuries later). Macbeth and his wife Gruoch donated land and money to the church. When Macbeth went on a pilgrimage to Rome he threw money at every beggar he saw.

In Rome he met up with Earl Thorfinn of Orkney.

The islands and the northern parts of Scotland still belonged to the Vikings, so the Earl wasn't exactly in Macbeth's good books. But like all world leaders

Long time no see, Eh, Thorfinn?

when they're out for a jaunt, they acted like buddies.

48

PILGRIMAGES

IT WAS COMMON FOR PEOPLE FROM ALL WALKS OF LIFE TO GO ON PILGRIMAGES IN THE MIDDLE AGES. THEY MADE THE JOURNEY (OFTEN DIFFICULT AND DANGEROUS) TO A HOLY PLACE IN THE HOPE THAT GOD WOULD PARDON THEIR SINS.

JERUSALEM IN THE HOLY LAND AND ROME, WHERE THE POPE LIVED, WERE FAVOURITE DESTINATIONS. CLOSER TO HOME, PEOPLE TRAVELLED AROUND SCOTLAND TO VISIT HOLY PLACES LIKE ST. ANDREWS OR THE ISLAND OF IONA.

THESE EVENTS COULD BE A BIT OF A BASH. PILGRIMS OFTEN WENT IN GROUPS – RATHER LIKE PACKAGE TOURS – OR MET UP WITH OTHER PILGRIMS ALONG THE ROUTE. THEY WOULD GET TOGETHER FOR A MEAL AND A LAUGH, TELL EACH OTHER STORIES AND SING RUDE SONGS.

When Macbeth got back from Rome someone was waiting for him – the dead king Duncan's son looking for revenge. Another battle (Lumphanan), another dead king (Macbeth) and another new one (Malcolm III).

MALCOLM WAS KNOWN AS CANMORE – BIG HEAD. PERHAPS THIS JUST MEANT 'LEADER' OR MAYBE HIS HEAD <u>WAS</u> BIG!

49

ACTUALLY, BEFORE MALCOLM HAD TIME TO RECOVER FROM BATTLE, SOMEONE ELSE HAD SLIPPED ONTO THE THRONE. IT WAS LULACH, MACBETH'S STEPSON. HE WAS KNOWN AS LULACH THE FOOL AND PERHAPS HIS MOTHER, GRUOCH, HAD EGGED HIM ON. HE ONLY LASTED A FEW MONTHS BEFORE THERE WAS A LITTLE INCIDENT WITH A KNIFE BETWEEN THE RIBS IN A QUIET CORNER...

Nice fit!

Malcolm wasn't the type to sit quietly with a good book (he couldn't read or write). 'Keep 'em afraid' could have been his motto as he set out with an army in search of sport. The Mormaers of Moray were the first to feel his softening-up tactics. He then invaded England, as he was sure the border could be pushed a little further south. Bad news for the people in the north of England who had their villages burnt, crops destroyed and were themselves dragged off as slaves.

Then, in 1066, an event in the far south of England changed things. William the Conqueror had arrived. William became king of England and he didn't take too kindly to the Scots rampaging round the top part of his kingdom. He came north with his army.

50

The two kings met at Abernethy. William smiled a predatory smile, Malcolm suddenly became co-operative and signed when William told him to do so.

PEACE TREATY
I   I AGREE TO STOP INVADING ENGLAND.
II   I AGREE TO BECOME KING WILLIAMS 'MAN' - MEANING WILLIAM IS A MORE IMPORTANT KING THAN ME AND WHAT HE SAYS, GOES.
III I AGREE TO GIVE MY SON DUNCAN TO WILLIAM AS A HOSTAGE AND IF I START ANY FUNNY BUSINESS, DUNCAN COPS IT.
     SIGNED:

Now, in one way Malcolm was very different from previous Scottish kings – he had lived in England for fifteen years and had picked up lots of English habits as well as learning to speak English (Gaelic was the language that most people spoke in Scotland).

That was fine for people who lived south of the River Forth (whose families had been Angles), but those in the north (descended from Scots and Picts) were suspicious of Malcolm's fancy English ways.

They became even more hostile when he married an English lady. When William the Conqueror invaded England, many people fled north to Scotland. Among them were Edgar the Aetheling (who should have been the next king of England) and his two sisters. Malcolm married one of them, Margaret.

Margaret was a very religious and severe woman. She was well educated and had been brought up in the civilized royal courts of Hungary and England. She bossily told Malcolm there would have to be some changes in her new home.

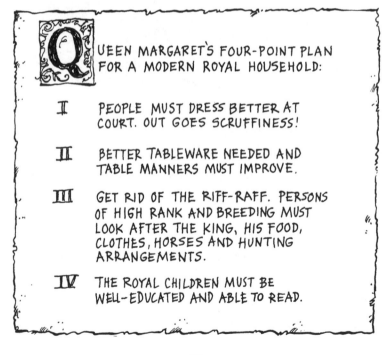

QUEEN MARGARET'S FOUR-POINT PLAN FOR A MODERN ROYAL HOUSEHOLD:

I   PEOPLE MUST DRESS BETTER AT COURT. OUT GOES SCRUFFINESS!

II   BETTER TABLEWARE NEEDED AND TABLE MANNERS MUST IMPROVE.

III   GET RID OF THE RIFF-RAFF. PERSONS OF HIGH RANK AND BREEDING MUST LOOK AFTER THE KING, HIS FOOD, CLOTHES, HORSES AND HUNTING ARRANGEMENTS.

IV   THE ROYAL CHILDREN MUST BE WELL-EDUCATED AND ABLE TO READ.

All these changes made the people in the north of the kingdom shake their heads in despair. To add insult to injury, Margaret gave her sons English names.

Malcolm agreed to all these changes. He had a tender side and every morning he lovingly touched Margaret's books, which he wasn't able to read.

PEOPLE WANTED AT COURT—
WELL-DRESSED AND
WELL-MANNERED.

PEOPLE NOT WANTED
AT COURT— THOSE
NEEDING SHOES AND
HAIRCUTS.

However, fighting was still the sport of kings. Malcolm took to his old ways and went off with an army to annoy the English. This time he and his eldest son were killed, and Margaret died of grief shortly after.

The problem now for Scotland was that Malcolm had left too many sons – Edmund, Edgar, Alexander and David. He also had another son, Duncan, from a previous marriage. All these sons had their eyes on the throne of Scotland, and the country was almost going to split apart in their attempts to get it. Who was going to make the first move?

They were pipped at the post by their Uncle Donald, Malcolm's brother (known as Donald Ban – White Donald; he was sixty, perhaps he had white hair). He hadn't been very keen on his brother's English ways and he got a lot of support from the people in the north of the country. He installed himself in Edinburgh Castle and had himself crowned Donald III.

Duncan was next to have a go. He was the hostage who had been taken by William the Conqueror. He had lived for some time at the English court, so his English pals gave him an army. He marched north, Donald fled.

Edmund was next. He teamed up with his Uncle
Donald and once more the northern supporters
came along, full of anti-English feeling. Duncan was
defeated and killed.

Donald and Edmund split the kingdom between
them. Donald ruled the north, Edmund the south –
until Edgar arrived. The English had supplied him
with an army, too, and he turfed Donald and
Edmund off their thrones. (So that he wouldn't
cause any more trouble, Uncle Donald's eyes were
plucked out. Who needs enemies with a family like
this?)

Edgar would never have got anywhere without the English army because he was a quiet and peace-loving man. During his reign he lost more of the west of Scotland to the Vikings because he couldn't be bothered going across there to sort things out. He wrote a note to the Viking boss which went something like this ...

Dear Magnus Barelegs,
Though Scotland really belongs to me, in the interests of peace and safety, I'll let you have all the bits of land you can sail round in your ship.
yours, Edgar K. of S.

So Magnus added every island to his territory, and just as a little extra, he had his ship dragged across the narrow bit of land at Tarbert on Loch Fyne, thus getting the Mull of Kintyre, too.

Only another twenty minutes and it's ours!

In spite of all the bloodshed of these times there was a gentler side to life ...

MONKS PRODUCED BEAUTIFUL BOOKS. THEY WERE HAND-WRITTEN ON VELLUM (CALFSKIN) AND DECORATED WITH PICTURES IN COLOURED INKS.

The peaceable Edgar arranged that his two remaining brothers should share the kingdom when he died. Alexander became King Alexander I (of the northern half) and David was in charge of the south. Soon, Alexander was gone, too, and David became king of all Scotland.

Which of the following is the worst behaviour?
a) Playing with matches in the Motte?
b) Reading in the Reredorter?
c) Being limp in the Lists?

KINGS DAVID I, MALCOLM IV, WILLIAM I

David was forty-four when he became David I of Scotland. He reigned for twenty-nine years, which gave him time to put the country into some sort of order.

Now, communications and trade between European countries were on the increase. Gossip got around. The last thing a king wanted was to hear that his court or his country was regarded as a bit of a joke.

I've just been to Scotland on business – scruffy little country!

My dear, the manners at the king's table are just awful!

Tell me more!

David wanted his country to be as modern as any other, so English and French ideas were on his shopping list. He'd lived in England for some time and had got friendly with many Anglo-Norman nobles. (These were the descendants of the Normans who had come with William the Conqueror in 1066.)

59

These Anglo-Normans were expert fighters, so crafty David invited many of them to Scotland and gave them gifts of land. He knew they'd terrify the wits out of the locals, wouldn't stand any nonsense and would keep the place in order. So it was good-bye to any Scots landowners who didn't see eye-to-eye with David.

(Many of these Anglo-Normans were going to play their part in Scotland's story, but by that time their Anglo-Norman names had become Scottish – de Brus became Bruce and FitzAllan became Stewart.)

A LORD NEEDED A PLACE TO LIVE IN. IT HAD TO BE SAFE AND IT HAD TO BE IMPRESSIVE, SO HE WOULD CONSTRUCT A MOTTE AND BAILEY. THESE WERE THE FIRST KIND OF CASTLES TO BE BUILT IN SCOTLAND.
THE MOTTE WAS A MOUND OF EARTH FOR THE LORD'S HOUSE TO SIT ON.
THE BAILEY WAS A FORTIFIED AREA ENCLOSING SMALLER BUILDINGS.
GATES

Don't drop the Lord's soup this time!

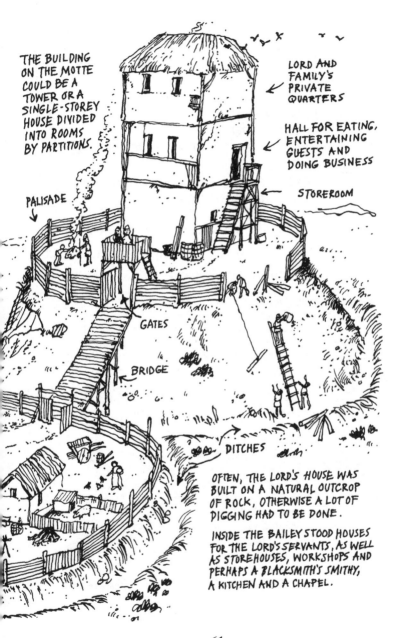

THE BUILDING ON THE MOTTE COULD BE A TOWER OR A SINGLE-STOREY HOUSE DIVIDED INTO ROOMS BY PARTITIONS.

LORD AND FAMILY'S PRIVATE QUARTERS

HALL FOR EATING, ENTERTAINING GUESTS AND DOING BUSINESS

STOREROOM

PALISADE

GATES

BRIDGE

DITCHES

OFTEN, THE LORD'S HOUSE WAS BUILT ON A NATURAL OUTCROP OF ROCK, OTHERWISE A LOT OF DIGGING HAD TO BE DONE.

INSIDE THE BAILEY STOOD HOUSES FOR THE LORD'S SERVANTS, AS WELL AS STOREHOUSES, WORKSHOPS AND PERHAPS A BLACKSMITH'S SMITHY, A KITCHEN AND A CHAPEL.

61

There were several important things a king needed:

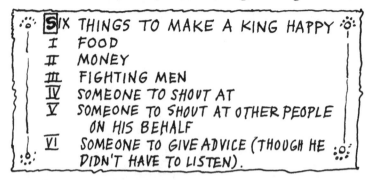

```
SIX THINGS TO MAKE A KING HAPPY
  I   FOOD
  II  MONEY
  III FIGHTING MEN
  IV  SOMEONE TO SHOUT AT
  V   SOMEONE TO SHOUT AT OTHER PEOPLE
       ON HIS BEHALF
  VI  SOMEONE TO GIVE ADVICE (THOUGH HE
       DIDN'T HAVE TO LISTEN).
```

To solve this, David introduced a nifty new arrangement that kings were using elsewhere; it was called the Feudal System in which everyone had a place.

THE KING GAVE LANDS TO HIS NOBLES. THESE LORDS OR EARLS BECAME THE KING'S VASSALS.

You may hold my land but you must help me in battle, court and council.

I swear to be faithful and serve you.

THE LORD HAD TO KEEP THE PEACE ON HIS LANDS. HE MAY HAVE HAD THE HONOUR OF A SPECIAL JOB AT COURT – PERHAPS LOOKING AFTER THE KING'S HORSES OR HIS HUNTING FALCONS. HE WAS EXPECTED TO PROVIDE FIGHTING MEN IF THE KING WENT TO WAR.

THE NOBLES ALSO GAVE LANDS TO OTHERS WHO THEN
BECAME *THEIR* VASSALS. MANY OF THESE PEOPLE HAD SPECIAL JOBS.
THEY MAY HAVE WORKED AS STEWARDS IN THEIR LORDS' HOUSES OR
THEY MAY HAVE BEEN ARMOURERS, BLACKSMITHS OR BREWERS.
THEY HAD TO PROVIDE THEIR LORD WITH AN ARMED MAN IN
THE EVENT OF WAR. THEY ALSO PAID RENT, EITHER IN MONEY
OR IN FOOD— THINGS LIKE SHEEP, CHICKENS OR GRAIN.

THESE PEOPLE IN THEIR TURN
LEASED SOME OF THEIR
ESTATES TO PEASANTS WHO
FARMED THE LAND AND WERE
EXPECTED TO GO INTO BATTLE
FOR THEIR LORD OR KING.

THE HUSBANDMEN OWNED THE
BIGGEST PORTION OF LAND AND
THEY MIGHT LEASE SOME SMALLER
BITS TO THE PEOPLE AT THE
BOTTOM OF THE PILE – THE
COTTARS. THE COTTARS OFTEN
HAD TO DO A BIT OF EXTRA
MANUAL LABOUR TO MAKE ENDS
MEET.

Malcolm encouraged monks to come and build monasteries in Scotland. Monks provided various services as well as a gentle side to life. They could read and write, and taught others to do the same. They knew about herbal medicines and cures, and could care for the sick and the poor. Monasteries

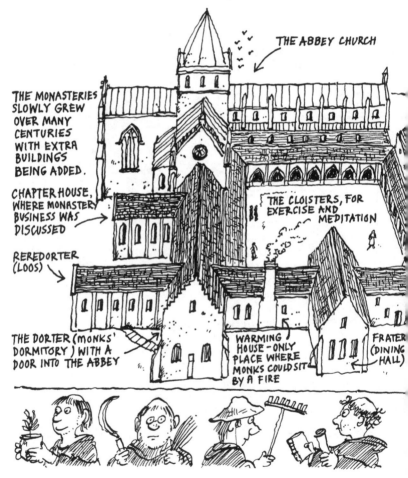

THE ABBEY CHURCH

THE MONASTERIES SLOWLY GREW OVER MANY CENTURIES WITH EXTRA BUILDINGS BEING ADDED.

CHAPTER HOUSE, WHERE MONASTERY BUSINESS WAS DISCUSSED

THE CLOISTERS, FOR EXERCISE AND MEDITATION

REREDORTER (LOOS)

THE DORTER (MONKS' DORMITORY) WITH A DOOR INTO THE ABBEY

WARMING HOUSE - ONLY PLACE WHERE MONKS COULD SIT BY A FIRE

FRATER (DINING HALL)

not only acted as hospitals but also as places where weary travellers could find a bed for the night.

The king gave the monks land which included farms, coal mines and fishing rights. As people in these times were very religious they liked to make sure of their place in heaven by giving generous gifts to the church or leaving the church something in their wills when they died. The monasteries became very rich.

INFIRMARY (HOSPITAL)

GUEST QUARTERS

LAYBROTHERS' QUARTERS. THEY HELPED WITH MONASTERY DUTIES BUT WERE NOT MONKS

ABBOT'S HALL

KITCHENS, BAKEHOUSE, BREWHOUSE, ETC.

Several times during the next fifty years Scotland was going to narrowly escape being swallowed up by England. The Scottish kings should have had a motto: Don't Meddle in English Affairs. But they didn't, and that led to trouble.

The Scots had always claimed that the northern counties of England belonged to them. David decided to get them back, went south with an army, but was defeated by the English led by the feisty old archbishop of York (in those days a battling bishop was common). This could have been bad for Scotland. Luckily, the English king had enough other troubles without bothering about tiresome Scots.

Yes, yes, take what you want but just leave me in peace!

Though defeated, the Scots got what they came for – Northumberland, Cumberland and Durham.

THEY WERE LOST AGAIN WHEN DAVID'S GRANDSON BECAME KING. MALCOLM IV WAS ONLY ELEVEN WHEN HE WAS CROWNED AND YOUNG KINGS ALWAYS GET HASSLE FROM GROWN-UPS. THE NEW ENGLISH KING, HENRY II, WAS MAKING AGGRESSIVE NOISES - SO GOODBYE NORTHUMBERLAND, CUMBERLAND AND DURHAM.

Give them back, Sire, or we're done for!

Malcolm was dead by the age of twenty-six and his brother William became king. He was yet another monarch who wasn't happy unless he was swinging a sword and he had plenty of time to do it, as he reigned longer than any other Scottish king – forty-nine years.

Now the English king had fallen out with his eldest son, so William made a deal with this son who was bent on revenge.

I'll help you become king of England if you give me back Northumberland, Cumberland and Durham.

Done!

William went south with his army. He stopped to besiege the town of Alnwick, and while he was there he received some good news and some bad news.

First the bad news – an English army was drawing near. Caught off guard, William was chained to his horse and dragged off to meet the English king. Now even worse (and embarrassing) news – the English king, Henry II, laid out his terms.

In return for your freedom, you must recognize me as your overlord. You are henceforth my vassal and you must do nothing without my permission!

No doubt, feeling furious, William had to agree.

KNIGHTS WERE THE MOST SKILLED FIGHTERS IN BATTLE. THE SONS OF NOBLES WENT THROUGH A SPECIAL CEREMONY TO BECOME A KNIGHT.
A KNIGHT HAD TO SHOW BRAVERY ON THE BATTLEFIELD AND CONSIDERATION FOR THE WEAK OFF IT.

BY NOW, KNIGHTS USED SO MUCH ARMOUR IN BATTLE IT WAS DIFFICULT TO TELL WHO WAS WHO, SO A TUNIC WITH AN EMBLEM ON IT WAS WORN OVER THE ARMOUR AS A DISTINGUISHING MARK.

WHEN NOT RIDING INTO BATTLE KNIGHTS PRACTISED (AND SHOWED OFF) IN TOURNAMENTS. THESE COMPETITIONS WERE HELD ON A BIT OF GROUND CALLED THE LISTS WHERE KNIGHTS TILTED AT ONE ANOTHER WITH LANCES OR FOUGHT HAND TO HAND. yee-hah!

68

But now the good news – Henry died. Even better news was to follow. Henry's son Richard was now king of England and he was a Crusades fanatic. All he wanted to do was go to the Holy Land and fight to free Jerusalem, the Holy City, from the hands of the Turks. In fact, he was very rarely at home. All this cost money, of course.

Hey, William, I'm a bit short of cash for my next crusade. Any chance of a donation?

Let's do a deal!

So William bought back Scotland's freedom.

Although the feudal system was now used in most of Scotland, the mountainous far west and north were still wild, independent places. The clan chiefs and the Vikings ran things their own way. William decided to tidy things up. He went round the country fighting furiously until all those with a glint of disobedience in their eyes were put in their place, and the Vikings were pushed into the sea (but not off the islands). The king's power now stretched from the River Tweed to the Pentland Firth.

Can wild horses give you a split personality? Should head-lice be kept out of your lunch? Does a king in his underpants mean the end?

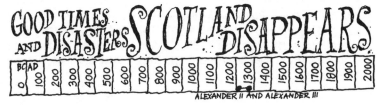

GOOD TIMES AND DISASTERS SCOTLAND DISAPPEARS

BC AD 0 | 100 | 200 | 300 | 400 | 500 | 600 | 700 | 800 | 900 | 1000 | 1100 | 1200 | 1300 | 1400 | 1500 | 1600 | 1700 | 1800 | 1900 | 2000

ALEXANDER II AND ALEXANDER III

By this time, if your dad was king, then it was likely you would be next on the throne. William's son became Alexander II and his son in turn became Alexander III.

Both kings were no-nonsense types who wanted a bit of peace in the country. Bloodshed was out – except if you were king, that is. Alexander's methods of keeping the peace weren't delicate. If there had been newspapers around at the time their headlines might have read ...

KING HAS REBELS' SEVERED HEADS DISPLAYED AT COURT

KING ORDERS NORTHERN NUISANCES EACH TO LOSE ONE HAND AND ONE FOOT

TROUBLEMAKERS TIED TO WILD HORSES AND TORN IN TWO

It may sound harsh, but it was the way of doing things in those days. The townsfolk of Edinburgh found the wild horse show very entertaining.

ALEXANDER WAS A KEEN CASTLE BUILDER. HE KNEW THAT CASTLES DOTTED AROUND THE COUNTRY, FILLED WITH HIS MEN, WOULD HELP TO KEEP THE PEACE. MANY CASTLES WERE NOW BEING BUILT OF STONE AND WERE IMMENSELY STRONG. THEY WERE USUALLY IMPROVED AND ENLARGED OVER THE CENTURIES.

MAIN TOWER WHICH INCLUDED THE LORD'S PRIVATE APARTMENTS, HIS WIFE'S APARTMENTS, GUEST ROOMS AND THE GREAT HALL FOR ENTERTAINING AND EATING.

STRONG GATEWAY PROTECTED BY TOWERS, A WOODEN DOOR OR IRON GATE

DRAWBRIDGE CLOSED IN TIMES OF DANGER

DUNGEON OR PIT, OFTEN BELOW GROUND

GARDEROBE OR LOO. WASTE FELL DOWN INTO A PIT.

72

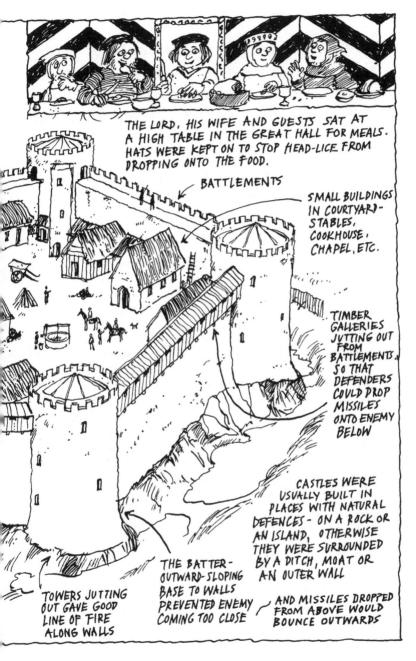

THE LORD, HIS WIFE AND GUESTS SAT AT A HIGH TABLE IN THE GREAT HALL FOR MEALS. HATS WERE KEPT ON TO STOP HEAD-LICE FROM DROPPING ONTO THE FOOD.

BATTLEMENTS

SMALL BUILDINGS IN COURTYARD - STABLES, COOKHOUSE, CHAPEL, ETC.

TIMBER GALLERIES JUTTING OUT FROM BATTLEMENTS, SO THAT DEFENDERS COULD DROP MISSILES ONTO ENEMY BELOW

CASTLES WERE USUALLY BUILT IN PLACES WITH NATURAL DEFENCES - ON A ROCK OR AN ISLAND, OTHERWISE THEY WERE SURROUNDED BY A DITCH, MOAT OR AN OUTER WALL

THE BATTER- OUTWARD-SLOPING BASE TO WALLS PREVENTED ENEMY COMING TOO CLOSE

AND MISSILES DROPPED FROM ABOVE WOULD BOUNCE OUTWARDS

TOWERS JUTTING OUT GAVE GOOD LINE OF FIRE ALONG WALLS

More than anything, Alexander wanted to get the Vikings out of the bits of Scotland they still held – the islands. He set out with an army to do just that, but only got as far as Oban where he fell ill and died.

Alexander III was only eight when he became king, so some of the nobles governed the country for him. Adults were always a problem for a boy king because they tended to get bossy and argumentative. Things got worse when the English king stuck his nose into Scottish affairs. He felt he could do this because his daughter had married Alexander (when he was ten).

THE NOBLES BEGAN TO DIVIDE INTO GROUPS, EACH WANTING TO INFLUENCE THE YOUNG KING. SOME POWERFUL FAMILIES EVEN RESORTED TO A COMMON PRACTICE OF THE TIME – KIDNAPPING. YOU CAN HAVE MORE INFLUENCE ON THE KING IF HE'S LOCKED IN YOUR SPARE ROOM.

It must have been a relief for Alexander when he reached twenty-one and he could rule by himself.

But more trouble came from another king – Hakon of Norway, leader of the Vikings. He decided to teach Scotland a lesson for the hassle the Vikings had been given. He sailed into the Firth of Clyde with a fleet of two hundred ships.

Now it was September and Alexander knew that this was a month of gales, so he kept Hakon talking until he got what he wanted – a ferocious storm which wrecked most of Hakon's fleet.

Hakon was defeated at the Battle of Largs and sailed away in a huff. From that day he knew he had lost the islands of the west (though the Vikings still hung on to Orkney and Shetland).

MANY PEOPLE WERE NOW LIVING IN TOWNS OR BURGHS.
THESE BURGHS USUALLY GREW UP NEAR CASTLES, MONASTERIES,
SEAPORTS OR RIVER-CROSSINGS.

PEOPLE IN TOWNS DIVIDED THEMSELVES INTO DIFFERENT CLASSES.

THE BURGESSES. THEY WERE THE
WEALTHY MERCHANTS, THOUGH THEY
HAD TO BE READY TO FIGHT FOR
THEIR KING IF NECESSARY. THEY
ACTED AS TOWN COUNCILLORS,
ARRANGED TOWN GUARDS AND
COLLECTED TAXES.

THE CRAFTSMEN - LIKE SMITHS,
BUTCHERS, GLOVE-MAKERS, ARMOURERS,
SHOEMAKERS, ETC. EACH TRADE
KEPT TO A SEPARATE PART OF TOWN
AND STREET NAMES OFTEN
INDICATED WHO WORKED THERE -
E.G. - 'CANDLEMAKERS' ROW'.

APPRENTICES. EACH CRAFTSMAN
TOOK ON A BOY TO LEARN A TRADE.
AT THE END OF THEIR TRAINING
THEY HAD TO MAKE A TEST-PIECE
- A BOOT OR SADDLE OR POT, FOR
INSTANCE. IF THEY PASSED THIS
EXAM THEY COULD BECOME CRAFTSMEN
THEMSELVES.

UNFREEMEN. THEY WERE THE
POOREST PEOPLE WHO HAD FEW
RIGHTS. THEY WORKED AS
LABOURERS OR SERVANTS.

BURGH COMMON
(FOR GRAZING ANIMALS)

CHURCH

BURGH ACRES
(FOR GROWING
VEG.)

BOOTH
OR
SHOP

LOO

OPEN
DRAIN

MUCK

GRAVEL
OR WOVEN
BRANCH
PATH

MUCK

GATE,
CLOSED
AT
NIGHT

77

Just when things were going well for Scotland, it all turned sour. Alexander's wife and all his children died. A year later, Alexander was thrown from his horse and killed.

Alexander's nearest heir was three years old and living in Norway. She was Margaret, the child of Alexander's daughter (now dead) who had married the Norwegian king. Meanwhile, six guardians were chosen to look after the country, but it was difficult to keep control. Now there was a whole string of nobles claiming royal blood in their veins and wanting to be king. The English king, Edward I, saw his chance for a bit of meddling and gave some advice ...

Things didn't go to plan. Little Princess Margaret (known also as the Maid of Norway) died on her way to Scotland.

Things looked bleak for Scotland. Then the quarrel-some nobles made an unfortunate decision – they turned to the English king for help.

Sure, I'll get you out of this mess – on one condition...

... Recognize me as overlord of Scotland and put all your castles into my keeping.

So Scotland's castles were filled with English soldiers and Edward got on with choosing the next Scottish king. He chose John Balliol.

FAMILY TREES

Now, let me see... We want someone co-operative.

Poor John was to be given the nickname 'Toom Tabard' (Empty Coat) and, caught between a rock and a hard place, he managed to make the messy situation worse.

He was bossed around by the Scottish nobles on one side and the English king on the other; then he made a fatal mistake – he signed a treaty of friendship with England's enemy, France.

King Edward was furious. He stormed north and rampaged around Scotland, burning, killing, torturing. (Edward gained a nickname, too – the Hammer of the Scots.)

John Balliol was humiliated, made to bow before Edward in his vest and pants before being dragged off to England.

Edward took some other things, too.

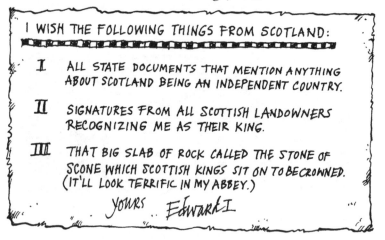

I WISH THE FOLLOWING THINGS FROM SCOTLAND:

I   ALL STATE DOCUMENTS THAT MENTION ANYTHING ABOUT SCOTLAND BEING AN INDEPENDENT COUNTRY.

II   SIGNATURES FROM ALL SCOTTISH LANDOWNERS RECOGNIZING ME AS THEIR KING.

III   THAT BIG SLAB OF ROCK CALLED THE STONE OF SCONE WHICH SCOTTISH KINGS SIT ON TO BE CROWNED. (IT'LL LOOK TERRIFIC IN MY ABBEY.)

YOURS .. Edward I

As far as Edward was concerned, he had wiped Scotland off the map.

What would you do to strike terror into your enemy:
a) Put a beak through his breastplate?
b) Hit him on the head with a horse?
c) Tell him his skin would make a lovely waistcoat?

A DYNAMIC DUO and THE FIGHT FOR INDEPENDENCE

BC AD | 0 100 200 300 400 500 600 700 800 900 1000 1100 1200 1300 1400 1500 1600 1700 1800 1900 2000

Scotland was in a sorry state. English governors now looked down from the castles on to towns filled with English soldiers and officials. To make matters worse, many Scottish nobles supported the English king and what he had done.

> Actually, I own several estates in England, so one has to be careful about taking sides... let sleeping dogs lie and all that...

Then one day, in the town of Lanark, there was an incident. The son of a local gentleman was walking up the street when he was taunted by an Englishman. Out came a sword. Result: One dead Englishman. As punishment, the town sheriff had the young man's house burnt to the ground. Unfortunately, his wife was inside. Result: One dead sheriff. Then widespread fighting broke out in the town. Result: The young man found himself master of the town backed up by a crowd of supporters.

81

The young man's name was William Wallace and these events opened his eyes to what had happened to his country. Now his one wish was that Scotland should be independent; so he and his men took over another town, and another, then a castle or two. Support grew until he found himself besieging Dundee with an army.

The English top brass in Scotland decided enough was enough. The Earl of Surrey marched forth with his men, and the two armies met on either side of the River Forth at Stirling. At the Battle of Stirling Bridge, the English were routed, the Scots triumphant.

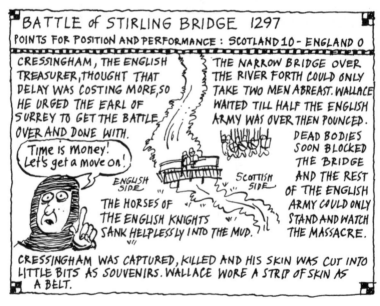

BATTLE of STIRLING BRIDGE 1297
POINTS FOR POSITION AND PERFORMANCE: SCOTLAND 10 - ENGLAND 0

CRESSINGHAM, THE ENGLISH TREASURER, THOUGHT THAT DELAY WAS COSTING MORE, SO HE URGED THE EARL OF SURREY TO GET THE BATTLE OVER AND DONE WITH.

Time is money! Let's get a move on!

ENGLISH SIDE

THE HORSES OF THE ENGLISH KNIGHTS SANK HELPLESSLY INTO THE MUD.

THE NARROW BRIDGE OVER THE RIVER FORTH COULD ONLY TAKE TWO MEN ABREAST. WALLACE WAITED TILL HALF THE ENGLISH ARMY WAS OVER THEN POUNCED.

DEAD BODIES SOON BLOCKED THE BRIDGE AND THE REST OF THE ENGLISH ARMY COULD ONLY STAND AND WATCH THE MASSACRE.

SCOTTISH SIDE

CRESSINGHAM WAS CAPTURED, KILLED AND HIS SKIN WAS CUT INTO LITTLE BITS AS SOUVENIRS. WALLACE WORE A STRIP OF SKIN AS A BELT.

It seemed that Wallace was going to succeed in his aims, but his luck ran out. King Edward of England had been busy thumping the French across the Channel, but now he returned and marched for Scotland. The two armies met at Falkirk; although Wallace's men fought bravely, they were no match for the 'Hammer of the Scots'. Defeated, Wallace escaped and kept a low profile. But he was a wanted man. Someone told the English exactly where to find him.

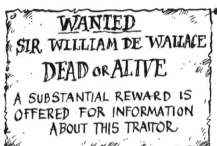

He was taken to London as a traitor, executed, and cut up into small bits. Parts of his body were displayed on poles in several Scottish towns as a dire warning to anyone else who had ideas about independence.

SOLDIERS of the WARS of INDEPENDENCE

HORSES HAD TO BE STRONG TO CARRY A KNIGHT IN ARMOUR.

PIKEMEN COULD PULL KNIGHTS FROM THEIR HORSES THEN STAB THEM.

BEAKED OR HAMMER-HEADED AXES COULD SMASH THROUGH ARMOUR.

84

PEASANTS AND FARMERS WOULD JOIN BATTLE WITH ANY WEAPON THEY COULD FIND—SCYTHES, FORKS, CLUBS, ETC.

GIANT AXE WIELDED BY A KNIGHT.

THE SKILFULL ENGLISH ARCHERS DEVASTED THE SCOTS AT THE BATTLE OF FALKIRK.

SCOTTISH SPEARMEN FORMED THEMSELVES INTO SQUARES CALLED SCHILTRONS— LIKE A GIANT PORCUPINE.

85

Within a year of Wallace's death another champion of Scottish independence had appeared. He was a descendant of King David I and his name was Robert Bruce, Earl of Carrick.

Up till now, Bruce's loyalties were a bit suspect. He owned estates in England as well as Scotland and had often fought in support of the English king.

But now a free Scotland, with himself as king, was his aim. He was crowned at Scone in front of a handful of supporters. The Countess of Buchan placed the crown on his head.

But that act made him English enemy number one and for a year Bruce played a game of cat and mouse with his enemies. English soldiers scoured the country for his whereabouts. There were informers ready with news, and ships kept watch along the coasts.

But if you can't get your man, you can get the next best thing. For instance …

INTERESTING THINGS TO DO WHILE WAITING TO GET YOUR MAN

* KILL HIS BROTHERS.
* IMPRISON HIS WIFE AND SISTERS.
* ARREST THE COUNTESS OF BUCHAN FOR HAVING THE IMPUDENCE TO PUT THE CROWN ON BRUCE'S HEAD. THEN THROW HER INTO A DUNGEON. BETTER STILL, STICK HER IN A CAGE LIKE AN ANIMAL IN A ZOO AND PEOPLE COULD COME AND GAWP AT HER.

Well, all these things Bruce's enemies did.

Disheartened, Bruce slipped away to an island and laid low. One of his surviving brothers, Edward, was with him and he persuaded Bruce to strike for freedom once more.

Bruce landed on the Ayrshire coast and soon defeated the Earl of Pembroke's army at Loudon Hill. Then news came that King Edward, 'Hammer of the Scots' was on his way north ...

Do I have to do everything myself?

... only to die on the journey. His son, the new king Edward II was a hopeless character and could be ignored. There was nothing to stop Bruce now. Within seven years he had captured every castle in Scotland except one.

Now, when Robert Bruce besieged a castle, he liked to batter it into submission.

EASI-SIEGE CATALOGUE PAGE 1

ALL THE LATEST MODELS. TERRIFIC BARGAINS.

SIEGE TOWER

TREBUCHET OR CATAPULT. COMES WITH NET FOR HOLDING ROCKS OR DEAD ANIMAL HOLSTER. (WE RECOMMEND PUTRID HORSE – SPREADS DISEASE QUICKLY AND EFFECTIVELY.)

BATTERING RAM

FRESH HIDES FOR DRAPING OVER SIEGE MACHINERY – EFFECTIVE AGAINST FIRE.

FLOATING, FOLDING BRIDGE

PORTABLE SHIELDS

His brother Edward thought this was a terrible waste of a good castle. He preferred patient starvation of the people inside. When he laid siege to the last castle in English hands, Stirling, he made an agreement with the governor.

If an English army doesn't come to help you by midsummer day, you must surrender the castle to us!

Agreed!

Perhaps Edward Bruce thought the English would never come north after so much Scottish success, but they did come. King Edward arrived with a huge army exactly on midsummer day.

20,000 English faced only 7,000 Scots across the Bannock Burn. One impatient English knight, Sir Henry de Bohun, caught sight of Bruce in front of his army and saw a chance to finish him off. Lance at the ready, he galloped furiously towards Bruce. At the last moment, Bruce neatly sidestepped on his horse, de Bohun went flying by – with a battleaxe stuck in his skull. It was a bad omen.

At the Battle of Bannock Burn the English were seriously defeated.

The English king fled to the safety of Stirling Castle.

The king rode on to Dunbar where he took a boat to safety.

The battle wasn't the end of the troubles. Fighting between English and Scots went on here and there for another fourteen years.

At one point some of the barons tried to find peace another way. They met at Arbroath and signed the Declaration of Arbroath. The Pope was going to get this in his post – a plea to an important person asking for independent Scotland to be recognized.

> ... so long as a hundred of us remain we are minded never a whit to bow beneath the yoke of the English. It is not for glory, riches or honour that we fight, it is for liberty alone.

Just a year before Bruce died, a treaty was signed between Scotland and England at Northampton. It was supposed to bring peace at last ...

... but it didn't. Robert's son David was only five when he became king. He spent a lot of his time abroad but he eventually ruled Scotland well. If David had kept a diary it might have read something like this:

> Dumbarton Castle. I'm not allowed to govern the country yet as I'm too young. The trouble is my Guardians keep getting killed...

... that's four I've lost.
There's a lot of fighting between the Scots and the English.

FRANCE   I've been sent to France for safety because there is still a lot of fighting at home. It's nice here. France is very posh. We watch the jousting every day.

Scotland   I'm old enough to run things now. I've decided to deal with the English once and for all, so I'm taking an army south.

ENGLAND   I made a bit of a mess of the battle. I got an arrow in the head which hurts a lot. Now I'm a prisoner in England but King Edward III and me get on just fine. It's very comfy here at the English court.

SCOTLAND   When I was in England, this terrible plague came which they called the BLACK DEATH because you come out in nasty black boils all over then you drop dead. The Scots laughed their heads off at this and called it the FOUL DEATH OF THE ENGLISH, but now the death has come here and they say that a third of the population has died.

I was only set free by the English on payment of a ransom. To pay this, I had to raise the taxes in the burghs. They weren't happy with this, so I said, in return, the Burgesses could come and take part in parliament.

The nobles and churchmen in parliament said they could deal with things on their own and didn't want any riff-raff in. But I said, like it or lump it.

Then they said I could pay the ransom myself if I didn't spend so much and they complained that I had picked up too many expensive habits in foreign courts.

Then I had a brilliant idea — as I had no heir, a really peaceful solution would be for my friend the KING of ENGLAND, or his son, to become KING OF SCOTLAND when I die. They all got really annoyed at this and said "over our dead bodies!" What did I say wrong?

If you are dished up with a bull's head for dinner do you:

a) Say you'll stick to cheese,

b) Ask for the horns as a souvenir,

c) Suddenly remember you have an appointment elsewhere?

TROUBLESOME KINGS AND STRONG BARONS · JUST WHO IS IN CHARGE HERE?

BC/AD	100	200	300	400	500	600	700	800	900	1000	1100	1200	1300	1400	1500	1600	1700	1800	1900	2000

THE FIRST STEWARTS

The job of Steward to the Royal Household was one of the most important in the kingdom. It was handed from father to son and the family was so proud of the title that they eventually took Steward – or Stewart – as their surname. David II had no children, so it was his nephew, Robert Stewart, who became king. The Stewarts were going to rule Scotland for centuries to come – and England, too.

Robert II was middle-aged by the time he became king. The English were busy elsewhere, so cross-border wars were out for the moment. However, there was trouble brewing at home – the nobles were becoming a bit too powerful.

OVER THE NEXT THIRTY YEARS THEY CREATED PRIVATE ARMIES, ACQUIRED MORE LAND AND TITLES. TAXES WENT UNCOLLECTED, CRIMES WENT UNPUNISHED AND PARLIAMENT HAD NO POWER TO DO ANYTHING ABOUT IT.

I wouldn't even trust my granny!

The next king, Robert III, wasn't any better – and he knew it. He had such a low opinion of himself that he asked to be buried in a dung-hill when he died.

Enter the Duke of Albany, the king's brother. He was made Guardian of the kingdom since a kick from a horse had made the king an invalid.

Albany was just beginning to enjoy his power when the queen decided that Prince David, her eldest son, was old enough to be Guardian.

Exit Prince David. The jealous Albany had him kidnapped and locked up in a castle where he soon mysteriously died. Now the king feared for his younger son, James. He packed him off to France for safety. But James's ship was captured by pirates, who very kindly handed over the prince to the king of England, who promptly locked him up in the Tower.

On hearing the news, his miserable old dad died of grief and the Duke of Albany, smiling with satisfaction, was once more in charge.

95

IN SPITE OF ALL THE TURMOIL, LIFE WENT ON AS USUAL...

THE MARKET (MERCAT) CROSS WHERE IMPORTANT PROCLAMATIONS WERE MADE.

HEADS (OR OTHER BITS) OF CRIMINALS AND TRAITORS WERE DISPLAYED HERE.

THE TOLBOOTH ACTED AS A COUNCIL CHAMBER, LAW COURT AND PRISON.

MARKET TRADING BEGAN AT THE RINGING OF A BELL.

A WRONGDOER IN THE STOCKS.

TOWNSFOLK GOT THEIR EARLY MORNING ALARM CALL ON THE BAGPIPES.

PEOPLE WHO COMMITTED MINOR CRIMES HAD TO SIT HERE WEARING A PAPER HAT. FOR INSTANCE, A BAKER WHO BAKED BAD BREAD WOULD HAVE TO SIT WITH ONE OF HIS LOAVES TIED AROUND HIS NECK.

THE CHURCH TOWER SOMETIMES DOUBLED AS A GAOL.

CHURCHYARDS WERE USED FOR DRYING WASHING, KEEPING ANIMALS AND DUMPING RUBBISH. IT WAS ABOUT THE ONLY PLACE WHERE YOUNG MEN AND WOMEN COULD MEET.

PUBLIC ENTERTAINMENT WAS PROVIDED BY MINSTRELS, ACTORS, ACROBATS AND MUSICIANS.

INSPECTORS CHECKED THE QUALITY OF GOODS IN THE MARKET.

STREETS WERE FILTHY AND FILLED WITH ROAMING ANIMALS.

97

Albany died, yet it was not until James was thirty that the English let him go. The Scots had to pay for his release, though the English didn't quite call it a ransom ...

James had learned quite a few things while in captivity in England. He was good at painting, drawing, music and writing poetry. He was also an athlete and liked to impress people with his skill in archery and strength events. He was keen to impress people in other ways, so he built a big palace at Linlithgow.

He had learned a thing or two about running a country, too – not all of them nice.

First Task: Cut your enemies down to size, preferably by removing their heads.

The Duke of Albany's family were first to go. James didn't like these power-greedy people. They were rounded up (including women and children) and thrown in gaol. The more dangerous ones were executed.

Other troublesome nobles went the same way. Lucky ones lost their lands, unlucky ones their heads.

Ordinary folk didn't escape. James passed lots of laws which kept them under control.

THINGS TO DISCUSS AT TODAY'S COUNCIL MEETING:

I   AFTER-HOURS DRINKING — MUST BE STOPPED — LET DECENT CITIZENS SLEEP IN PEACE.

II   DRESS CODE NEEDED — WE CAN'T HAVE EVERYONE JUST WEARING WHAT THEY WANT — EXCEPT THE KING, OF COURSE.

III   FIRE-FIGHTING — TOO MANY TOWNS BURNING DOWN — MUST ORGANIZE FIRE-FIGHTING.

IV   FOOTBALL — NOISY, UNCOUTH, DANGEROUS — MUST BE STOPPED.

V   ARCHERY. INSTEAD OF BREAKING EACH OTHER'S SKULLS PLAYING FOOTBALL, YOUNG PERSONS SHOULD PRACTISE ARCHERY — THEN THEY COULD BREAK THEIR ENEMY'S SKULL FROM A SAFE DISTANCE.

James's ruthless methods created two things: a stable kingdom and a good few enemies. A small group of nobles now hated the King's guts and wanted to see a sword sticking in them. They plotted.

They came for him while he was staying in Perth. James saw the torches in the night and knew what was up. One of the court ladies barred the door with her arm (ouch, nasty). James lifted some floorboard and dropped into the cellar; but the exit was blocked (to stop tennis balls rolling in, it's said). James met a grisly death in the darkness.

James II was only six when he became king on the death of his father. This meant he was surrounded by adults squabbling for power. The governor of Stirling Castle removed James from Edinburgh, then the governor of Edinburgh Castle had him kidnapped and brought back.

But then the two governors teamed up against a greater enemy.

There was no family as powerful as the Douglases. Their idea of a family day out was to go and barbecue an English castle. They were feared and admired, and because they had royal blood in their veins, they were dangerous.

The two governors invited the Earl of Douglas to Edinburgh Castle.

> To the Earl of Douglas
> Do come to dinner. Midday, sharp. Don't wear anything special.
>   Yours, Livingstone and Crichton H.M's Castle Governors.

At the end of the meal a black bull's head was placed on the table. This was a sign that someone was soon going to die. It was the Earl of Douglas's head that was soon rolling across the courtyard after the 'Black Dinner'.

There were plenty more dangerous Douglases, though. When James was fifteen he decided to invite the new Earl of Douglas to Stirling Castle for a friendly chat. But they ended up arguing and another Douglas lay dying – this time stabbed by the king himself. Not a good move as far as James was concerned.

He would have to break the power of the Douglases before they broke him, so he battered them into submission by attacking their castles with cannons (a fairly recent invention, especially ones with wheels which could be moved around).

By the time he was thirty James had managed to get his kingdom under some sort of control; however, a cannon was going to be his undoing. While besieging Roxburgh Castle, a cannon exploded near the king and blew him to smithereens. No doubt the Douglases were laughing in their graves.

Like his father, James III was only a boy when he became king. More adult arguments.

The nobles managed to come to some agreement about who James should marry. They chose the daughter of the Norwegian king. As part of the marriage deal, Scotland got Orkney and Shetland.

THE KING MAY HAVE THOUGHT HE WAS NOW IN CONTROL OF ALL SCOTLAND, BUT THE CLAN CHIEFS IN THE WEST STILL LIKED TO DO THINGS THEIR OWN WAY. THE CHIEF OF THE MACDONALDS CALLED HIMSELF THE LORD OF THE ISLES AND CONSIDERED HIMSELF IMPORTANT ENOUGH TO SIGN A TREATY OF FRIENDSHIP WITH THE ENGLISH KING. SCOTTISH KINGS SOON LOST PATIENCE WITH THIS NONSENSE AND THE MACDONALDS HAD TO FORFEIT THEIR LANDS

ORKNEY AND SHETLAND – PREVIOUS OWNER – THE KING OF NORWAY – NOW PART OF SCOTLAND.

LORDSHIP OF THE ISLES

STIRLING

LINLITHGOW EDINBURGH

Tell His Lordship to behave – or else!

HUNTING WAS THE SPORT OF KINGS AND QUEENS. LARGE AREAS OF LAND WERE SET ASIDE AS HUNTING FORESTS FOR THE PLEASURE OF THE MONARCH. WHEREVER THE KING WAS IN SCOTLAND, THERE WAS USUALLY A HUNTING PARK NEARBY. FALKLAND PALACE IN FIFE WAS ORIGINALLY BUILT AS A HUNTING LODGE. IT ALSO HAD A TENNIS COURT IN WHICH THE KING COULD SHOW OFF HIS FITNESS AND SKILL. THE GAME WAS A VERSION CALLED REAL (ROYAL) TENNIS, ORIGINALLY PLAYED WITHOUT RACKETS.

When James was old enough to rule by himself his nobles were in for a great disappointment. They got the cold shoulder. James much preferred the company of a small circle of court favourites.

What do they see in him?

The nobles soon tired of the king's arrogant ways and hung some of his cronies over the side of Lauder Bridge (by their necks).

A few years later some of the nobles decided to skip James and move on to his son instead. They proclaimed the fifteen-year-old boy the new king. Father and son met with their supporters to fight it out. At the Battle of Sauchieburn the old king lost his crown and his life.

Is oral hygiene of royal interest? Will an Italian with a lute end up as a sieve? Should a queen decide a queen's for the chop?

BC	AD	100	200	300	400	500	600	700	800	900	1000	1100	1200	1300	1400	1500	1600	1700	1800	1900	2000
0																					

TWO MORE STEWARTS AND A STUART (FRENCH SPELLING)

The world was now changing rapidly. Columbus had sailed across the Atlantic. Merchants were travelling round the world in their ships. People were inventing new things, making scientific discoveries, creating wonderful works of art.

James IV was the right kind of king for these times. He was handsome, energetic, athletic and he spoke several languages. He was also a brilliant self-publicist.

He liked to show how in touch with the times he was.

He liked to show he cared.

KING TAKES A GREAT INTEREST in DENTISTRY, ALCHEMY and THE POWERS of FLIGHT

Open wide!

THE CLANK 'N' CLINK KING

KING JAMES HAS VOWED TO WEAR AN IRON BELT FOR THE REST OF HIS LIFE TO SHOW REMORSE FOR FIGHTING AGAINST HIS FATHER

He liked to prove how athletic he was.

He liked to show how gallant he was …

… and how he was just one of the lads.

He liked to be seen around the country …

… and he liked to stay at home.

KING with a SPRING. KING JAMES LIKES TO LEAP INTO THE SADDLE OF HIS HORSE WITHOUT TOUCHING THE ANIMAL.

KING with a CLANG. KING JAMES LIKES TO TONE UP HIS MUSCLES BY REGULARLY HAMMERING AN ANVIL.

KING LEADS THE LADIES AT COURT A MERRY DANCE! NO BEAUTY IS SAFE FROM HIS CHARMS.

CHANCE for a CHINWAG. KING TURNS UP AT HIGHLAND FIRESIDE for a CHAT.

JAMES THE JUST. KING TRAVELS ROUND his REALM MAKING SURE LAWS ARE KEPT and LISTENING to PEOPLE'S PROBLEMS.

…and another thing…

King says: 'EDINBURGH IS CAPITAL of SCOTLAND' HE LAYS THE FIRST BRICK OF WHAT WILL BE HIS POSH PALACE AT HOLYROOD.

Above all, he enjoyed creating a colourful splash.

KING (29) MARRIES MARGARET TUDOR (13) OF ENGLAND IN MAGNIFICENT WEDDING

NEW FACES IN TOWN - MANY NEW TRADES AND PROFESSIONS WERE SPRINGING UP.

THE PRINTER. PRINTING HAD JUST BEEN INVENTED IN EUROPE. BOOKS WERE NOW AVAILABLE FOR LARGE NUMBERS OF PEOPLE. THE FIRST BOOKS PRINTED IN SCOTLAND – 1503.

THE SEACAPTAIN SCOTLAND NOW HAD A NAVY OF ABOUT TWENTY SHIPS.

THE SCHOOLTEACHER AND THE UNIVERSITY PROFESSOR NOBLES AND MERCHANTS WERE ENCOURAGED TO SEND THEIR SONS TO SCHOOL. THERE WERE NOW THREE UNIVERSITIES IN SCOTLAND.

FOREIGN CRAFTWORKERS MANY PEOPLE CAME FROM EUROPE TO WORK IN SCOTLAND, ESPECIALLY IN THE CLOTH-TRADE AND FISHING.

THE PROFESSIONAL SOLDIER AND THE ARTILLERY-MAKER – BETTER THAN EXPECTING A FARMER TO COME FROM HIS FIELDS WITH HIS BOW AND ARROW.

ACTORS, SINGERS AND MUSICIANS MONARCHS WANTED PEOPLE WHO COULD PROVIDE LAVISH ENTERTAINMENT.

109

Scotland was a more peaceful and well-ordered place. There was no trouble from England, as the miserly King Henry VII didn't like wars – they cost money. But things changed when his son became king. The aggressive Henry VIII was spoiling for a fight. His taunts that Scotland actually belonged to him made James see red. He raised an army and marched into England.

James was clever but impatient. He ordered his men to charge too soon. The Scots were disastrously defeated at the Battle of Flodden and James was killed along with many of his nobles. The big take-over by the English could have happened there and then, but luckily the English had other problems, so Scotland was left alone. (Phew.)

So now there was another young king – James V was only seventeen months old – which brought the usual old problem:

James's mother made things worse by re-marrying – one of the ambitious Douglas family, and James's stepfather enjoyed keeping the young king under his thumb.

Well, little king, you won't be going far for a while!

By the age of sixteen James managed to escape the clutches of the Douglases. It was Revenge time; if you were a Douglas, best to lie low, or even leave.

But there was other business to attend to. What was he to do about this new craze sweeping Europe – the Reformation?

THE REFORMATION

MANY PEOPLE WERE GETTING A BIT FED UP WITH THE CATHOLIC CHURCH. THEY THOUGHT THAT BISHOPS AND MONKS WERE GETTING SEEDY AND GREEDY – AND ANYWAY, WHY SHOULD THE POPE TELL THEM WHAT TO DO? THESE PEOPLE WANTED RELIGION REFORMED AND MODERNIZED. IN FACT, KING HENRY VIII OF ENGLAND HAD ALREADY DITCHED THE POPE AND PROCLAIMED HIMSELF HEAD OF THE CHURCH IN ENGLAND.

We PROTEST!

We are Protestants!

We want to be able to read the Bible in our own language – not that lousy old Latin

So … James came to an arrangement with the Pope …

> Dear Pope,
> I can assure you that I have no intention of changing over to this Reformation lark. However, I'm a bit short of money, so a generous donation would certainly secure my support for you.
>
> Yours, in anticipation   James

He got his money. Money was also on his mind when it came to choosing a wife. Both the French and the English kings had offered him a bride. James wanted one that came with cash – but who to choose without-

out causing offence? He chose French. The miffed Henry VIII sent a small army up to Scotland to burn a few villages. It took a lot of persuasion from James to get his nobles to retaliate.

When an army did get together it was hardly worth the bother. Result: Another embarrassing Scottish defeat – the Rout at Solway Moss.

Sad and ill, James took to his bed. News then came that he had an heir at last – a baby girl. A week later, James was dead.

Scottish monarchs were getting younger and younger. James's daughter Mary was only a week old when she became Queen of Scots. Her kingdom was splitting apart again – this time religion was the cause. Should Scotland keep in with her old friend France (a Catholic country) or make friends with England (a Protestant country)?

There was a long cast-list of characters in this drama ...

ACT ONE

Henry VIII of England's part
Little Mary had been promised to Henry as a wife for his son (but Scotland might then become part of England). The marriage was broken off. Henry went ballistic. Bad move, Sire. Rough handling won't get you anywhere.

Mary of Guise's part (the Queen mum)
Mary sent her daugher off to France, where she was married to the French king's son (but would Scotland now become part of France?). Mary of G. put herself in change of Scotland. Tricky move, Madame. (She soon dies, anyway.)

Cardinal Beaton's part
Scotland was being overrun by Protestants. The
Cardinal wanted it to remain Catholic. It was he
who had broken off the marriage between little
Mary and Henry VIII's son. Bad move, Cardinal.
Murdered by Protestant rebels, his body was dan-
gled from his castle walls.

George Wishart's and John Knox's part's
They preached the Protestant message up and down
the country. Bad move, lads – still a lot of powerful
Catholics about. Wishart was burnt at the stake as a
heretic (along with a good few others) and Knox
was sent off to be a galley slave (he'll be back).

The nobles' part
The new religion was
catching on rapidly.
Now the Protestant
nobles started fighting
with the Catholic ones.

Parliament declares that Scotland is now officially a Protestant country.

The Protestants gained the upper hand. Parliament
was summoned to discuss the matter.

ACT II
Mary returned from France when she was eighteen.
Her husband – who had been king of France for less
than two years – had died.

114

John Knox's part, *again*

Although Scotland was now officially a Protestant country, Mary (a Catholic) would be allowed to follow her own religion in private. To Knox this was obnoxious. He and the Queen argued a lot.

Lord Darnley's part

Mary married Lord Darnley, handsome yet immature. They had a son. Mary soon tired of Darnley. She really went off him when he got mixed up in the murder of her secretary. Bad move, My Lord. You look childish when you're jealous.

Rizzio's part

He was an Italian musician who did Mary's paperwork. He became the Queen's favourite at court. Bad move, Signore. Enter a band of lords with knives. Rizzio came to a sticky end (56 wounds) on the palace floor.

115

The Earl of Bothwell's part

Darnley had been recovering from an illness at Kirk
o' Field, a house near Edinburgh. One night the
house blew up. Gunpowder had been placed in the
basement (how strange …). Darnley was dead. (Not
blown up but strangled – even stranger …). Bothwell
was blamed. He brought so many supporters to his
trial that the judges were
terrified to condemn him.
Bad move, My Lord.

Queen Mary's part

Mary was beautiful, charismatic but wilful. Things
had a habit of turning sour around her. Bothwell
abducted her from Edinburgh
and took her to his castle,
where she married him. Oh,
bad move, My Lady.

The Protestant lords' part

Enough was enough. The lords raised an army and
went off to meet Bothwell. His supporters deserted
him, so the match was off.
Bothwell slipped out of the
country. Mary was locked
up in Loch Leven Castle,
but her friends got her out.

(Chase Scene)

Her supporters were defeated at the Battle of Langside. Mary escaped into England.

The Queen of England's part
Elizabeth I was now queen south of the border. She didn't approve of Mary's behaviour, but she didn't approve of the rebellious Scots either. (They might give her own subjects ideas.) She knew that Mary had long had her eye on the English throne; in fact, because Elizabeth was child-less, it was Mary's son James who had the best claim to be Elizabeth's heir. Mary was one hot potato. Elizabeth kept her under house arrest for eighteen years. She would be dangerous on the loose; eventually she became dangerous alive.

Is this the wrong time to: a) Go on a kidnapping expedition with an earl, b) Try a Glencoe B and B, c) Buy a ticket for the trip-of-a-lifetime to South America?

117

THE MONARCH MOVES HOME ONE KING TWO KINGDOMS

BC	AD																			
0		100	200	300	400	500	600	700	800	900	1000	1100	1200	1300	1400	1500	1600	1700	1800	1900	2000

FIVE MORE STUARTS

James VI was only a year old when he was proclaimed king. Here we go again …

This time the squabbling nobles divided themselves into Queen Mary's supporters (Catholics) and James's supporters (Protestants).

While James was a child the country was ruled by earls who were called regents. First, the Earl of Moray (assassinated), then Lennox (assassinated), next Mar (died in bed, lucky him) and lastly Morton (executed).

Whoever held the king, held power. There were two ways to do this:

First method – the Subtle Approach – become the king's favourite at court. James had a soft spot for men who were flattering, witty and colourful.

118

THE LORD OF AUBIGNY WAS ONE OF THEM. HE WAS FRENCH BUT BELONGED TO THE STEWART (OR STUART) FAMILY. HE WAS A SMOOTH AND SLIMY OPERATOR. HE HAD BEEN SENT OVER TO SCOTLAND TO TRY AND GET MARY BACK ON THE THRONE. HE CERTAINLY HAD POWER OVER JAMES AS HE PERSUADED HIM TO EXECUTE REGENT MORTON AFTER SPREADING NASTY RUMOURS ABOUT THE EARL.

You showed *dazzling* skill at the hunt today, Sire!

Second Method – The No-Messing Approach – kidnapping the king. There were nine attempts to kidnap James.

THE EARL OF GOWRIE WAS THE MOST SUCCESSFUL AND HE MANAGED TO HOLD THE KING FOR A YEAR. HE MADE JAMES SEND AUBIGNY BACK TO FRANCE AND WANTED SCOTLAND TO BECOME A FRIEND OF PROTESTANT ENGLAND. JAMES EVENTUALLY ESCAPED AND GOWRIE LOST HIS HEAD. NO WONDER JAMES BECAME A WARY MAN. IT'S SAID HE ALWAYS WORE PADDED CLOTHES FOR FEAR OF ASSASSINATION.

James ruled the country himself from the age of sixteen. When he was thirty-seven, Queen Elizabeth I of England died; he was her nearest heir. The Queen wasn't keen on James (she called him 'that Scottish man'), but her chief minister had been writing to James in code, preparing him for the take-over.

119

So James VI of Scotland became James I of England as well, and his kingdom lay in two separate countries. He decided to move south to London. He travelled slowly, admiring the elegant English country houses and enjoying the hunting. He was a hunting fanatic. He would often arrive late at important meetings wearing his mud-spattered outdoor clothes and boots. James told the Scots he would visit them regularly but he came only once and spent most of the time ... hunting.

However, as king, he had one or two ideas which didn't go down very well ...

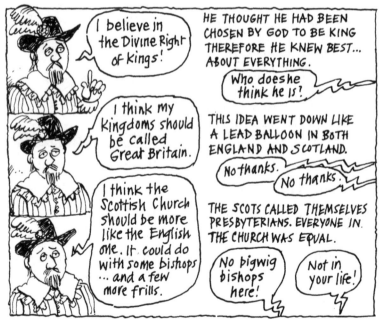

THE ENGLISH WERE RATHER SNOOTY ABOUT JAMES'S STRANGE ACCENT AND ODD IDEAS. IN THEIR OPINION, HE LACKED DIGNITY.

RELIGIOUS BELIEFS CAUSED PROBLEMS IN ENGLAND AS WELL AS SCOTLAND. SOME CATHOLICS TRIED TO ASSASSINATE JAMES BY BLOWING UP THE HOUSES OF PARLIAMENT IN THE 'GUNPOWDER PLOT'. THE PURITANS (LIKE THE SCOTS, WANTED THE CHURCH TO BE SIMPLER) WERE MAKING A NOISE, TOO, AND MANY LEFT IN DISGUST TO SETTLE IN AMERICA.

James was a well-educated, clever and wily man. He didn't stand on ceremony and liked to gossip and joke. In spite of his faults he knew how to control his people and brought peace and prosperity to his kingdoms.

The same can't be said for his son, Charles I. He was tactless, arrogant and distant.

Charles got up everyone's nose.

The English got so fed up with him that a civil war broke out between parliament (the Roundheads), who wanted to get rid of him, and the Royalists (Cavaliers), who supported him.

CHARLES had said...  Goodbye, Scotland!  ... AT THE AGE OF THREE (HE WAS THE LAST KING TO BE BORN IN SCOTLAND) WHEN HIS FATHER BECAME KING OF ENGLAND AND MOVED SOUTH.

CHARLES said... Hello, Scotland! ...WHEN HE CAME NORTH FOR HIS SCOTTISH CORONATION. THE STREETS OF EDINBURGH WERE SWEPT CLEAN OF FILTH AND THE BEGGARS WERE LOCKED UP. BRANCHES HUNG WITH FLOWERS DECORATED THE STREETS AND THE ROTTEN HEADS OF CRIMINALS DISPLAYED ON POLES WERE REMOVED. (NO ONE KNEW AT THE TIME THAT THE KING'S HEAD WAS SHORTLY GOING TO BE REMOVED, TOO.)

BUT THE SCOTS WERE APPALLED BY CHARLES'S FANCY CHURCH OF ENGLAND CORONATION SERVICE IN EDINBURGH.

All those fancy clothes and lace!

Can I not persuade you to have a few bishops?

How many times do we have to say it? We're Presbyterians!

CHARLES said... Goodbye, Scotland! ...WHEN HE WENT BACK SOUTH THEN THE SCOTS RUSHED TO SIGN A PETITION CALLED A COVENANT DEMANDING THAT THEIR CHURCH BE LEFT ALONE... AND A COVENANTERS' ARMY WENT OFF TO JOIN THE ROUNDHEAD SIDE IN THE ENGLISH CIVIL WAR.

Charles was tried for treason and lost his head. Now the Scots had to make a decision. Who did they want as head of state? The prospective candidates were ...

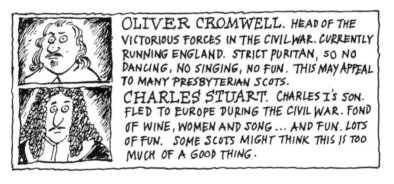

The Scots hankered after a king, so Charles was invited to Edinburgh and crowned as Charles II. Bad move. General Monck, Cromwell's hatchet man, arrives. Charles makes a quick exit.

If the Scots can't behave, they can't have a country. To show that Scotland was no longer an independent nation, Monck (just like Edward I) commanded the Scots to hand over their symbols of nationhood.

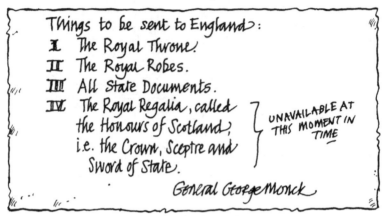

Things to be sent to England:
I   The Royal Throne.
II   The Royal Robes.
III All State Documents.
IV The Royal Regalia, called the Honours of Scotland; i.e. the Crown, Sceptre and Sword of State.

UNAVAILABLE AT THIS MOMENT IN TIME

General George Monck

The Honours had been taken to Dunottar Castle. The English besieged the castle, but the Honours were smuggled out and hidden under the floor of a nearby church.

Cromwell didn't last long and the monarchy was restored. But Scotland was of little importance to Charles II and his brother, James VII, who ruled after him.

In fact, life in Scotland was a bit unsettling. English religious services were forced on the people and everyone had to attend church, no excuses. If you were unhappy with this, there were persuasions.

THINGS TO DO TO SCOTTISH COVENANTERS...

1. FORBID OTHERS TO TALK TO THEM OR GIVE THEM WORK.
2. FORCE THEM TO GIVE LODGINGS TO SOLDIERS. THERE'S NOTHING LIKE AN UNCOUTH SOLDIER FOR WRECKING YOUR HOUSE AND FAMILY, SHOOTING YOUR COW, SPITTING IN YOUR PORRIDGE, ETC.
3. TRANSPORT THEM TO AMERICA.
4. APPLY THE BOOT. (SEE FIG. 1.)
5. SHOOT THEM ON THE SPOT.

FIG 1.

No wonder these were known as the 'Killing Times'.

THE BOOT—A NIFTY WOODEN FRAME INTO WHICH A LEG IS PUT. WEDGES ARE THEN HAMMERED IN CAUSING GREAT PAIN AND RATHER A MESS.

Covenanting ministers were not allowed to serve in church, so they held their services in the open air, with guards posted to warn of approaching soldiers. (On the other hand, the Covenanters weren't exactly a bundle of laughs. Prim and disapproving, they wouldn't accept ministers who hadn't signed their covenant.)

After a bit, something dawned on James VII – he was becoming very, very unpopular. He was a Catholic and both Scots and English suspected he wanted to turn them into Catholics, too.

Congratulations! You've just been voted least popular monarch.

ALTHOUGH WEALTHY SCOTS STILL
LIVED IN FORTIFIED TOWERS,
MANY WERE HAVING ELEGANT
HOUSES BUILT AS THE COUNTRY
WAS BECOMING MORE PEACEFUL.

THE GENTLEMAN OF THE HOUSE
MIGHT SEND HIS SON TO
UNIVERSITY, READ A NEWSPAPER
AND PLAY GOLF.
HIS LADY MIGHT COMMISSION
A FINE PORTRAIT, PLAY A
MUSICAL INSTRUMENT AND LOOK
AFTER HOUSEHOLD ACCOUNTS.

126

IN THE COUNTRY, POORER PEOPLE
LIVED IN MUCH THE SAME WAY
AS A CENTURY BEFORE. HOUSES
HAD THATCHED ROOFS AND
EARTH FLOORS.
LARGER AND MORE COMFORTABLE
BUILDINGS WERE APPEARING
IN TOWNS.

SWORD-CARRYING WAS SLOWLY DYING OUT BUT PEOPLE COULD
STILL BE BURNED FOR WITCHCRAFT. THE SCOTS LANGUAGE WAS
SLOWLY DISAPPEARING BUT GAELIC WAS STILL THE LANGUAGE
OF THE WEST.

127

Eventually, the English had the cheek to invite his daughter Mary (a Protestant) to become queen. As she and her Dutch husband William of Orange (plus a small army) arrived from across the Channel, James hastily departed in the opposite direction.

Scotland didn't see much of dull, humourless William; he never set foot on Scottish soil. However, one of the first things he did earned him a gold star – he approved of letting the Scots run their church the way they wanted; so at last, the Presbyterian church in Scotland was free from English meddling.

BUT HANG ON A MINUTE... CATHOLIC JAMES STILL HAD HIS SUPPORTERS. ONE OF THESE WAS VISCOUNT 'BONNIE' DUNDEE WHO HOPED HE COULD WIN BACK SCOTLAND FOR JAMES. HE GATHERED AN ARMY OF HIGHLANDERS AND MARCHED SOUTH. HE WAS MET BY THE NEW KING'S FORCES AT THE PASS OF KILLIECRANKIE, NEAR PITLOCHRY. THE HIGHLANDERS CHARGED - BUT THE KING'S SOLDIERS HAD JUST BEEN ISSUED WITH A NEW PIECE OF EQUIPMENT - THE BAYONET. WHILE THEY WERE FIGURING OUT HOW TO FIX THEM, THEY WERE CUT TO PIECES. IT WAS AN EMPTY VICTORY - DUNDEE WAS KILLED AND THE HIGHLANDERS, AFTER A SPOT OF LOOTING, MELTED AWAY INTO THE GLENS.

Hold part A and swivel part B against part C ... done that...

THANK YOU FOR CHOOSING THE BRUISER. BAYONET. PLEASE READ THE OPERATING INSTRUCTIONS:

William didn't want another rebellion like that, so a fort was built on the West Coast (named after the king, Fort William) and an army garrison was installed to keep an eye on the highlanders. Then the King added an extra safety measure.

> ## VERY IMPORTANT NOTICE
>
> ALL HIGHLAND CHIEFS MUST SWEAR ALLEGIANCE TO KING WILLIAM III BY THE FIRST DAY OF JANUARY 1692 OR BE CONSIDERED OUTLAWS AND LOSE THEIR LANDS. WE LOOK FORWARD TO SEEING YOU AT YOUR NEAREST ALLEGIANCE-SWEARING OFFICE.
>
> William

All chiefs swore allegiance in time, except for the Macdonald of Glencoe. He had left it a teensy bit late and when he arrived at Fort William …

Macdonald arrived at Inveraray three days after the deadline and swore allegiance. But a late allegiance was no allegiance at all as far as Secretary of State Dalrymple was concerned. He chose to make an example of the Macdonalds. Soldiers were quartered in all the Glencoe houses.

129

Thirty-eight men, women and children were killed when the soldiers struck. Other Macdonalds died in the snowy mountains as they tried to escape. The massacre of Glen Coe shocked the nation, but worse was to come – the Darien Disaster.

WHO WANTED A SWAMPY, STINKING, MOSQUITO-RIDDEN PIECE OF LAND IN CENTRAL AMERICA? THE SCOTS DID. BY LAW, SCOTTISH MERCHANTS WEREN'T ALLOWED TO TRADE WITH ENGLISH COLONIES AROUND THE WORLD. SOME MERCHANTS DECIDED THAT SCOTLAND SHOULD HAVE A COLONY OF ITS OWN. THEY HEARD OF A PIECE OF EMPTY LAND IN CENTRAL AMERICA, SO HUGE AMOUNTS OF MONEY WERE RAISED TO SEND SETTLERS TO DARIEN. THEY VERY QUICKLY DIED OF DISEASE, STARVATION AND ATTACKS BY THE SPANISH. THE IDEA WAS A DISASTER AND ALMOST RUINED SCOTLAND FINANCIALLY.

NORTH AMERICA

HOME

SPANISH COLONIES

CARIBBEAN SEA

DARIEN

PACIFIC OCEAN

MOSQUITOS

SPANISH COLONIES

SOUTH AMERICA

It may not have been the King's fault that these two disasters happened, but the Scots blamed him all the same. King William was not a very popular man.

Who do you think would be best to lead your rebellion: Mr Misfortune, Bobbing John or Betty Burke?

GOOD NEWS OR BAD NEWS? ONE PARLIAMENT TWO NATIONS

BC	AD 0	100	200	300	400	500	600	700	800	900	1000	1100	1200	1300	1400	1500	1600	1700	1800	1900	2000

QUEEN ANNE, THE LAST STUART - AND A FEW KING GEORGES

Now the future didn't look good for the Stuart dynasty. This is how things stood:

Queen Mary – dead
King William – dead

WILLIAM WAS KILLED WHEN HIS HORSE TRIPPED ON A MOLEHILL AND HE WAS THROWN OFF AND KILLED. MANY SCOTS WERE PLEASED ABOUT THIS AND USED TO DRINK A TOAST...

Here's to the little gentleman in black velvet!

Queen Anne (Mary's sister) – almost dead. Well, not exactly bursting with health. (She had to be carried to her coronation on a chair.)

Anne's children (all seventeen of them) – dead.

There had to be a suitable relation ready to become monarch should Anne die. The English Parliament did their research then passed an Act:

131

We proclaim the Act of Succession in which Sophie, Electress of Hanover in Germany, grand-daughter of James VI of Scotland and I of England (or one of her children) will become next monarch.

But they forgot to ask the Scots if this was okay with them. The Scottish Parliament went in the huff and passed its own Act …

We proclaim that we might accept a Hanoverian as next monarch … on the other hand … we might get our own bloke in. Depends.

So the English passed another Act …

We proclaim that all Scots are foreigners and none of their exports – cattle, coal or linen, shall be allowed into England!

People on both sides of the border began to get a bit worried – this bickering might turn into war. Then a bright spark came up with an idea:

So the English Parliament drew up the Act of Union.

The Scots could not make up their minds about this.

The Members of Parliament mulled over the official papers for three months before signing them. Thus, on the 1st of May, 1707, the Scottish Parliament disappeared.

Half the country cheered while the other half wept – and rioted; and eventually riot turned into rebellion.

The Earl of Mar had been keen on the Union, but now he changed his mind. He organized a hunting party on his estate, but it wasn't deer he had in his sights.

In 1715 the Earl gathered an army and raised his standard at Braemar. But the omens for this rebellion weren't good.

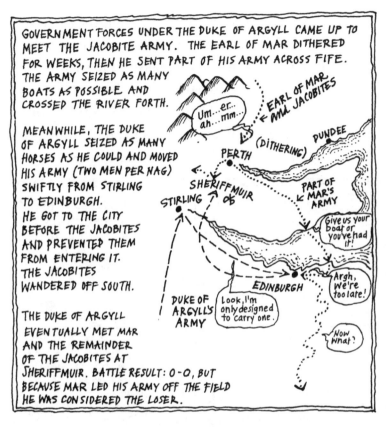

The rebels were called Jacobites (from the Latin word Jacobus = James), the rebellion became known as the 'Fifteen and it was all over in less than three months. James 'Mr Melancholy' Stuart arrived in Scotland too late for the show, and promptly went back to France again.

135

Thirty years later the Jacobites thought they'd have another go. This time the man applying for the post of leader had a bit more enthusiasm. He was James's son, Charles Edward Stuart, better known as Bonnie Prince Charlie. He pulled on his tartan togs and headed for Scotland. But was his rebellion going to be any more successful than the last one?

FRENCH IN A FLAP
THE FRENCH AGREED TO HELP BY SENDING 10,000 TROOPS, BUT THE FLEET CARRYING THEM GOT CAUGHT IN A FEROCIOUS STORM. THE SHIPS RETURNED TO PORT AND STAYED THERE.

TITCHY TASK FORCE
CHARLES ARRIVED ON THE WEST COAST OF SCOTLAND AND RAISED HIS STANDARD AT GLENFINNAN. HE HAD SEVEN MEN WITH HIM – HARDLY AN ARMY THAT WOULD SET THE HEATHER ALIGHT.

CHARMING CHARLIE
THE PRINCE WASN'T EXACTLY A LOCAL. HE HAD BEEN BROUGHT UP IN ITALY AND WHAT HE LACKED IN EXPERIENCE (HE WAS 25) HE MADE UP IN CHARM. SOON THE HIGHLANDERS AND THEIR CHIEFS WERE RUSHING TO JOIN HIM.

Who's for a bit of glory?

Charles set out at the head of his army. His progress was astounding. Within four months he had reached Derby. Across Europe people eagerly followed this daring adventure in their newspapers. What would happen next? It became a damp squib.

To his disappointment, Charles found there was no support for him in England. Best to beat a hasty retreat …

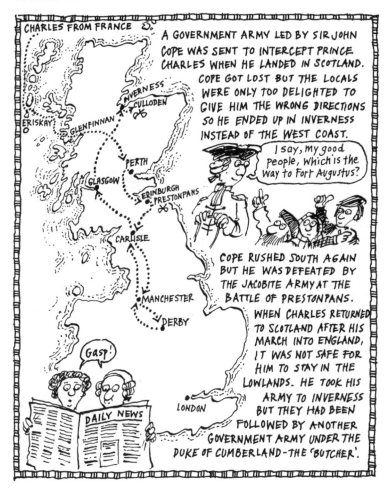

In the spring of 1746 the armies of Prince Charles and the Duke of Cumberland had arrived at either side of Culloden Muir.

Perhaps Charles ought to have done his homework and thought about a five-point plan on how to be successful on the battlefield:

1 *Surprise the enemy.* Charles did try this but too late. By the time Charles's men had tip-toed towards Cumberland's camp, dawn had broken and they had to scurry back.

2 *Don't let the enemy surprise you.* They did. Charles's men had only just got back to their own camp when word came that Cumberland had followed them.

3 *Make sure your men are fighting fit.* Charles's highland-ers were exhausted and starving.

4 *Make sure you have the right numbers.* A little on the short side here. Charles had around 5,000 men: Cumberland had almost twice that.

5 Make sure your men are trained and equipped.
Cumberland had trained soldiers with guns and cannons. The highlanders fought in the same way as they had done for centuries.

Result: A massacre. Dead highlanders lay in heaps on the battlefield. The remainder of the army fled.

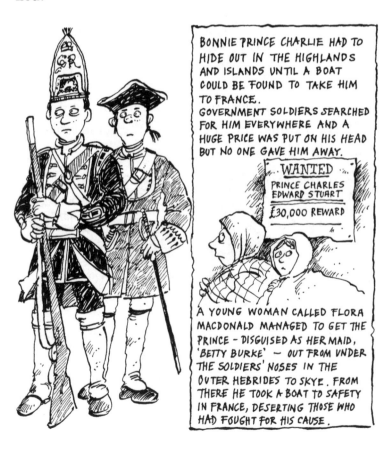

BONNIE PRINCE CHARLIE HAD TO HIDE OUT IN THE HIGHLANDS AND ISLANDS UNTIL A BOAT COULD BE FOUND TO TAKE HIM TO FRANCE.
GOVERNMENT SOLDIERS SEARCHED FOR HIM EVERYWHERE AND A HUGE PRICE WAS PUT ON HIS HEAD BUT NO ONE GAVE HIM AWAY.

WANTED
PRINCE CHARLES EDWARD STUART
£30,000 REWARD

A YOUNG WOMAN CALLED FLORA MACDONALD MANAGED TO GET THE PRINCE – DISGUISED AS HER MAID, 'BETTY BURKE' – OUT FROM UNDER THE SOLDIERS' NOSES IN THE OUTER HEBRIDES TO SKYE. FROM THERE HE TOOK A BOAT TO SAFETY IN FRANCE, DESERTING THOSE WHO HAD FOUGHT FOR HIS CAUSE.

Cumberland ruthlessly chased the remaining Jacobites. Nobles and chiefs were executed and their lands forfeited. Highlanders were shot or transported in their hundreds to America.

Culloden was the last battle to be fought on British soil. For a while, the English and the Scots looked at each other through narrowed eyes ...

But the Jacobites would soon be forgotten in the peace that followed.

Are pink tights the best thing to wear with tartan?
Can chips make you travel faster?
Is firewood now the best use for your spinning-wheel?

PEACE and PROSPERITY CULTURE AND CREATIVITY

BC	AD																			
0	100	200	300	400	500	600	700	800	900	1000	1100	1200	1300	1400	1500	1600	1700	1800	1900	2000

In 1822, King George IV paid a visit to Edinburgh. He was the first monarch to visit Scotland for 171 years.

GEORGE I, GEORGE II AND GEORGE III HADN'T BOTHERED MUCH ABOUT SCOTLAND. GEORGE I HADN'T BOTHERED MUCH ABOUT ENGLAND EITHER. HE WAS THE MAN WHO CAME OVER FROM HANOVER FOR THE JOB OF BRITISH MONARCH. HE DIDN'T SPEAK ENGLISH AND PREFERRED TO SPEND MOST OF HIS TIME BACK IN HANOVER. A 'PRIME MINISTER' WAS APPOINTED TO LOOK AFTER GREAT BRITAIN.

GEORGE, GEORGE, GEORGE...

...AND GEORGE

By now, the Scots had been allowed back their plaids and their pipes, so George IV dressed up to the nines for his visit. He wore full highland gear plus a pair of pink tights to modestly cover the royal legs. The city was in a festive mood.

About seventy years had passed since the 'Forty-five Rebellion, and Scotland had changed dramatically.

Out went the treeless landscape, big boggy bits and fields in thin, overworked strips ...

...IN CAME DRAINS AND DITCHES, WALLS AND HEDGES, LARGE, WELL-TENDED FIELDS, VARIETIES OF CROPS AND FORESTRY PLANTATIONS.

FARMING MACHINERY LIKE THRESHING MACHINES AND REAPERS SPEEDED UP FARM WORK.

MORE AND MORE SHEEP WERE APPEARING ON SCOTTISH HILLSIDES

THE HIGHLANDERS AND ISLANDERS FOUND THERE WAS A GREAT DEMAND FOR BEEF IN ENGLAND. THEY BROUGHT THOUSANDS OF THEIR CATTLE EVERY YEAR TO THE MARKETS AT CRIEFF AND FALKIRK ALONG ROUTES KNOWN AS 'DROVE ROADS'.

CRIEFF

FALKIRK TRYST

THE CATTLE WERE SHOD WITH METAL SHOES TO PROTECT THEIR FEET ON THE LONG JOURNEY.

142

Out went muddy tracks, pot-holed roads and difficult travel …

... IN CAME MR. JOHN MᶜADAM OF AYRSHIRE, THE CHIPS CHAMPION. HE KNEW A THING OR TWO ABOUT ROAD-BUILDING. HE INVENTED A NEW METHOD OF MAKING ROADS WITH STONE CHIPS WHICH PROVIDED A SMOOTH, HARDWEARING SURFACE.

THE CHIPS HAD TO BE THE RIGHT SIZE. THE ROAD-BUILDERS WERE ISSUED WITH TWO-INCH RINGS. EVERY STONE HAD TO BE SMALL ENOUGH TO PASS THROUGH THE RING.

MR MᶜADAM'S ROAD

SLOPED SO THAT WATER DRAINED AWAY

THE STONE CHIPS KNITTED TOGETHER UNDER THE WEIGHT OF THE TRAFFIC.

THOMAS TELFORD, SON OF A DUMFRIESSHIRE SHEPHERD WAS ANOTHER ROAD-BUILDER BUT HE ALSO BUILT BRIDGES, CANALS AND HARBOURS.

TRAVEL WAS BECOMING MUCH QUICKER. STAGE-COACHES SPED ALONG THE NEW ROADS THAT LINKED TOWNS AND CITIES.

GLASGOW-EDINBURGH EXPRESS

143

Out went slow manufacture by hand … in came fast manufacture by machine …

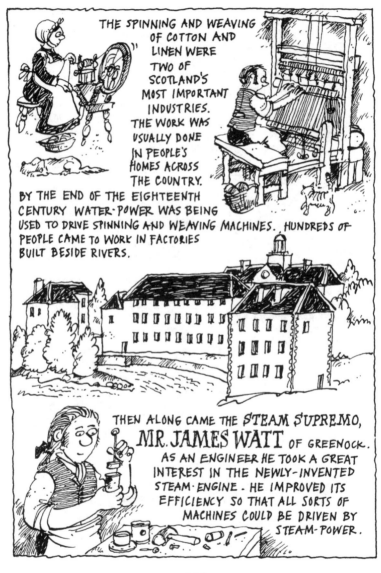

THE SPINNING AND WEAVING OF COTTON AND LINEN WERE TWO OF SCOTLAND'S MOST IMPORTANT INDUSTRIES. THE WORK WAS USUALLY DONE IN PEOPLE'S HOMES ACROSS THE COUNTRY.

BY THE END OF THE EIGHTEENTH CENTURY WATER-POWER WAS BEING USED TO DRIVE SPINNING AND WEAVING MACHINES. HUNDREDS OF PEOPLE CAME TO WORK IN FACTORIES BUILT BESIDE RIVERS.

THEN ALONG CAME THE *STEAM SUPREMO*, **MR. JAMES WATT** OF GREENOCK. AS AN ENGINEER HE TOOK A GREAT INTEREST IN THE NEWLY-INVENTED STEAM-ENGINE. HE IMPROVED ITS EFFICIENCY SO THAT ALL SORTS OF MACHINES COULD BE DRIVEN BY STEAM-POWER.

Out went tricky travel on water where ships were at the mercy of wind and tide …

ONE OF THE FIRST THINGS TO BENEFIT FROM STEAM-POWER WAS TRAVEL BY SEA.

IN CAME MR. WILLIAM SYMINGTON OF LEADHILLS AND MR. HENRY BELL OF LINLITHGOW, PRINCES OF PROPULSION. MR. SYMINGTON INVENTED A CARRIAGE DRIVEN BY STEAM AND THE FIRST STEAM-DRIVEN PADDLE-SHIP. MR BELL'S PADDLE-STEAMER 'COMET' WAS THE FIRST STEAM-DRIVEN SHIP TO RUN A PASSENGER SERVICE.

SHIPS NEED NO LONGER WAIT FOR THE WIND BUT LOTS OF COAL MINES WERE NEEDED TO PRODUCE THE COAL THAT MADE THE STEAM THAT DROVE THE NEW MACHINERY. MUCH LATER, THE EVENTS OF THIS TIME WERE GIVEN A NAME - THE INDUSTRIAL REVOLUTION. SCOTLAND WAS BECOMING A NOISIER PLACE.

The Scots had given up fighting. Instead, American students came to study at Scottish universities and Europeans visited Scotland to absorb the culture. Scotland was the 'in' place at the end of the eighteenth century ...

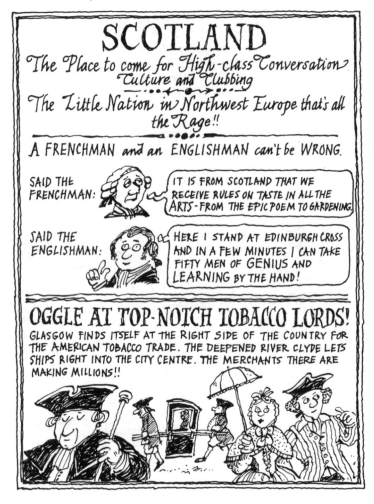

SCOTLAND

The Place to come for High-class Conversation Culture and Clubbing

The Little Nation in Northwest Europe that's all the Rage!!

A FRENCHMAN and an ENGLISHMAN can't be WRONG.

SAID THE FRENCHMAN: IT IS FROM SCOTLAND THAT WE RECEIVE RULES ON TASTE IN ALL THE ARTS - FROM THE EPIC POEM TO GARDENING.

SAID THE ENGLISHMAN: HERE I STAND AT EDINBURGH CROSS AND IN A FEW MINUTES I CAN TAKE FIFTY MEN OF GENIUS AND LEARNING BY THE HAND!

OGGLE AT TOP-NOTCH TOBACCO LORDS!

GLASGOW FINDS ITSELF AT THE RIGHT SIDE OF THE COUNTRY FOR THE AMERICAN TOBACCO TRADE. THE DEEPENED RIVER CLYDE LETS SHIPS RIGHT INTO THE CITY CENTRE. THE MERCHANTS THERE ARE MAKING MILLIONS!!

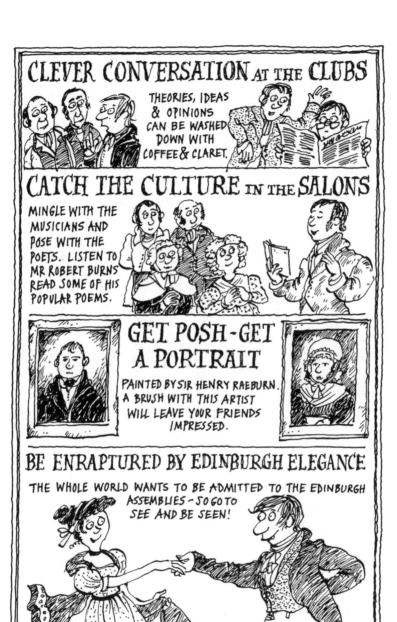

CLEVER CONVERSATION AT THE CLUBS

THEORIES, IDEAS & OPINIONS CAN BE WASHED DOWN WITH COFFEE & CLARET.

CATCH THE CULTURE IN THE SALONS

MINGLE WITH THE MUSICIANS AND POSE WITH THE POETS. LISTEN TO MR ROBERT BURNS READ SOME OF HIS POPULAR POEMS.

GET POSH - GET A PORTRAIT

PAINTED BY SIR HENRY RAEBURN. A BRUSH WITH THIS ARTIST WILL LEAVE YOUR FRIENDS IMPRESSED.

BE ENRAPTURED BY EDINBURGH ELEGANCE

THE WHOLE WORLD WANTS TO BE ADMITTED TO THE EDINBURGH ASSEMBLIES - SO GO TO SEE AND BE SEEN!

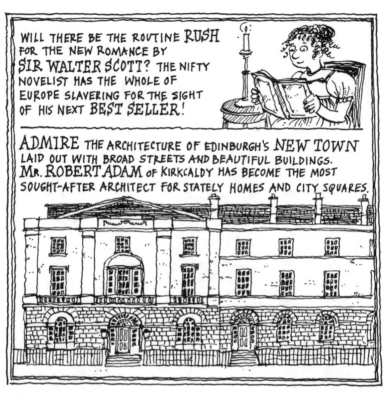

WILL THERE BE THE ROUTINE RUSH FOR THE NEW ROMANCE BY SIR WALTER SCOTT? THE NIFTY NOVELIST HAS THE WHOLE OF EUROPE SLAVERING FOR THE SIGHT OF HIS NEXT BEST SELLER!

ADMIRE THE ARCHITECTURE OF EDINBURGH'S NEW TOWN LAID OUT WITH BROAD STREETS AND BEAUTIFUL BUILDINGS. MR. ROBERT ADAM OF KIRKCALDY HAS BECOME THE MOST SOUGHT-AFTER ARCHITECT FOR STATELY HOMES AND CITY SQUARES.

Many Scots thought the Union was brilliant. Some even called their country North Britain and tried to get rid of their Scottish accents. Eager beavers went off to run the British Empire in the far-flung corners of the world.

Which of these is the most depressing situation?
a) A crofter when he hears loud baa-ing.
b) A bug sensing a poker is being heated.
c) A horse watching tram-lines being laid.

EITHER YOU HAVE IT OR YOU HAVEN'T... THE VICTORIAN AGE

BC	AD	100	200	300	400	500	600	700	800	900	1000	1100	1200	1300	1400	1500	1600	1700	1800	1900	2000
0																					

Who were you if an age had been named after you, you liked tartan on everything and had bought a highland estate for your hols?

Answer: Queen Victoria.

149

Who were you if you had just bought a first-class railway ticket, enjoyed shooting and fishing, and found highland games a great entertainment? Answer: A wealthy tourist or landowner.

RAILWAY LINES BEGAN TO THREAD THEIR WAY ACROSS THE COUNTRY AND REACHED INVERNESS BY 1863.
THEY BROUGHT RICH TOURISTS WHO CAME TO ADMIRE THE MAJESTIC SCENERY OR WATCH CABERS BEING TOSSED IN THE NEW FASHION FOR ORGANIZED HIGHLAND GAMES.
AFTER A SPOT OF PAINTING OR FISHING THERE WOULD BE A PICNIC AND A CHANCE TO HAVE THE HOLIDAY RECORDED BY THE LATEST INVENTION – THE CAMERA.

Say cheese!

WEALTHY LOWLANDERS AND ENGLISHMEN BOUGHT UP HUGE AREAS OF THE HIGHLANDS. THE PEOPLE WHO LIVED THERE DIDN'T FIGURE VERY HIGHLY IN THE SCHEME OF THINGS.

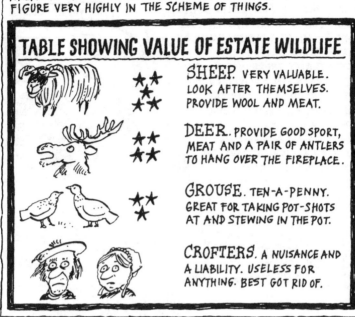

TABLE SHOWING VALUE OF ESTATE WILDLIFE

★★★★★ **SHEEP.** VERY VALUABLE. LOOK AFTER THEMSELVES. PROVIDE WOOL AND MEAT.

★★★★ **DEER.** PROVIDE GOOD SPORT, MEAT AND A PAIR OF ANTLERS TO HANG OVER THE FIREPLACE.

★★★ **GROUSE.** TEN-A-PENNY. GREAT FOR TAKING POT-SHOTS AT AND STEWING IN THE POT.

CROFTERS. A NUISANCE AND A LIABILITY. USELESS FOR ANYTHING. BEST GOT RID OF.

Who were you if you lived in a draughty hovel by the edge of a loch, near starvation, and perhaps with a one-way ticket to America? Answer: A crofter turned off the land by the estate landlord.

THE LANDOWNERS FORCED CROFTERS OUT OF THEIR HOMES TO MAKE WAY FOR SHEEP AND DEER. THE MASS REMOVAL OF PEOPLE BECAME KNOWN AS THE 'CLEARANCES'. THE CROFTERS HAD TO SCRATCH A LIVING AS BEST THEY COULD FROM POOR LAND BESIDE LOCHS OR THE SEA OR...

... THEY COULD SAIL TO NORTH AMERICA TO SEEK A BETTER LIFE OR DRIFT INTO THE CITIES TO TRY AND FIND WORK. MOST PEOPLE LEFT THEIR CROFTS PEACEABLY, BUT SOMETIMES THERE WAS TROUBLE AND POLICE OR SOLDIERS WOULD HAVE TO BE BROUGHT IN. EVENTUALLY THERE WAS A SERIOUS CONFRONTATION BETWEEN SOME CROFTERS ON SKYE AND THE GLASGOW POLICEMEN BROUGHT IN TO HELP WITH THE EVICTIONS, AND THE GOVERNMENT HAD TO PASS A LAW WHICH GAVE THE CROFTERS SOME SECURITY.

Are you not Donald McLeod's boy?

IN THE COUNTRYSIDE, MANY PEOPLE STILL LIVED IN THE SAME KIND OF HOUSES THEY HAD LIVED IN FOR CENTURIES.

MORE COMFORTABLE HOUSES COULD BE FOUND ON WEALTHIER FARMS AND IN TOWNS.

MECHANIZATION ON THE FARM MEANT LESS JOBS FOR FARMWORKERS.

Who were you if you shared a room with ten other people as well as rats and creepy-crawlies, suffered all sorts of illness and went to the loo in the back-yard? Answer: A slum-dweller in a big city.

THE POPULATION OF TOWNS AND CITIES WAS GROWING AS PEOPLE CAME TO WORK IN THE FACTORIES. LARGE FAMILIES HAD TO LIVE IN HOUSES OF ONE OR TWO ROOMS – ALONG WITH THE VERMIN. SMALL BUGS COULD BE CONTROLLED BY A HOT POKER JAMMED INTO CRACKS AND CREVICES IN WALLS OR FLOORBOARDS.

SIZZLE!

FIVE HUNDRED AND EIGHTY THREE!

THE STREETS AND BUILDINGS IN THE SLUMS WERE FILTHY AND STINKING. SOOT AND SMOKE FILLED THE AIR. CHILDREN WERE VERY LUCKY IF THEY HAD SHOES.

NORMAL   SHEER LUXURY

Who were you if you had bacon, tea, sugar and cakes for your tea, were saving up to buy a piano and nipped down to the library to get the latest adventure by Robert Louis Stevenson? Answer: A member of the new middle classes.

Until now, very few people had the right to vote for their town councillors and MPs. The voting system was a bit dodgy, too.

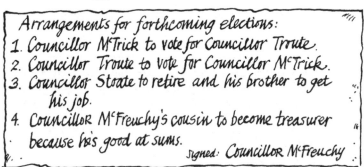

Arrangements for forthcoming elections:
1. Councillor McTrick to vote for Councillor Troute.
2. Councillor Troute to vote for Councillor McTrick.
3. Councillor Stoate to retire and his brother to get his job.
4. Councillor McFreuchy's cousin to become treasurer because he's good at sums.
Signed: Councillor McFreuchy

Reforms got rid of these cosy arrangements. Many more people were given the right to vote, though not women or the poor.

Councillors took their work more seriously.

155

Who were you if you had a 'marine villa' for holidays, went to the theatre regularly and had a huge conservatory full of tropical plants built on the side of your house? Answer: A rich businessman or factory-owner.

THE RICH HAD LARGE HOUSES BUILT FOR THEM BY FASHIONABLE ARCHITECTS. THERE WOULD HAVE BEEN ACCOMMODATION FOR SEVERAL SERVANTS AND A COOK, AND PERHAPS A HOUSE FOR THE COACHMAN IF THE OWNERS HAD A CARRIAGE AND HORSES.

GROCER

MANY OF THE RICH HAD A SECOND HOME BY THE SEA FOR THE SUMMER BUT PEOPLE FROM ALL WALKS OF LIFE LIKED TO GO TO THE COAST FOR A DAY OUT.

Ice Cream

The insides of houses were full of fussy decoration. Rooms were crammed with furniture, pot-plants and pictures. Towards the end of the century an architect called Charles Rennie Mackintosh changed all that by designing buildings in a new style called *Art Nouveau*.

Someone, somewhere, is still farming and fishing in Scotland, but now heavy industry is employing more people.

If it could be made in iron and steel, then Scotland made it.

Sometimes the workers went on strike for better pay and conditions; but they had to be careful or they'd get more than they bargained for ...

For the miserable supporters of this disruption I sentence them to one month's imprisonment... for those who resorted to violence – deportation to Australia ... and for the ringleaders – execution!

The end of the Victorian Age was electrifying! The new power put horses out of business and trains into tunnels; the Glasgow Underground whisked people quickly round the city in little carriages.

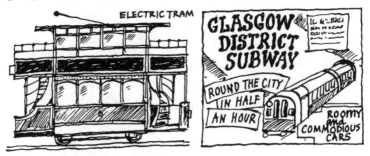

The Victorians thought big – big Empire and big ideas that made some people a lot of money. For many who worked to bring about these ideas, life was not so rosy.

Does the curry come with chips? Can snow become a satisfying experience? Will the stone ever stop travelling?

BC	AP	100	200	300	400	500	600	700	800	900	1000	1100	1200	1300	1400	1500	1600	1700	1800	1900	2000
0																					

Amazing new colourful things arrived with the twentieth century. It was hello to radio, dancehalls, jazz bands and cinemas. By the middle of the century it was hello to rock and roll, and goodbye to the gloom and misery of war.

During the First World War it was hello to hardship and shortages, and goodbye to the 74,000 Scots who died on the battlefields.

Women had to take the place of men in the factories and farms.

Hello! These women are as good as men in the workplace!

Let's say goodbye to discrimination, then! Allow us to vote!

AFTER THE FIRST WORLD WAR, WOMEN WERE ALLOWED EQUAL VOTING RIGHTS WITH MEN.

160

Not so many of the armed forces lost their lives in the Second World War, but the war came closer to home and civilians died.

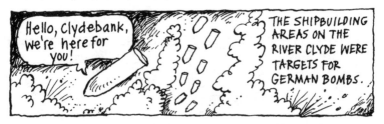

After the wars traditional industries collapsed. It was far cheaper to get things from abroad.

So it was goodbye to ...

and hello to ...

Scotland began to shrink (not in size) as modern communications and transport – electric trains, bridges, tunnels, motorways, aeroplanes, television, telephone – brought everyone closer together.

Scots had more free time for leisure …

Though for many, life wasn't getting better …

It was goodbye to unpopular landowners ...

It was hello to people from other lands ...

The twentieth century brought new political parties ...

It was goodbye, hello, goodbye, hello to that Stone …

And what will the future hold? Will the Loch Ness Monster turn out to be a Martian spy? Will a president of Scotland take her oath? Will Scotland slip under the ice again? Who knows …

List of Dates

End of the Ice Age – around 10,000 BC
People arrive in Scotland – around 6,000 BC
Farmers arrive – around 4,000 BC
Bronze Age – from around 2,000 BC
Iron Age – from around 700 BC
Romans in Scotland – AD 80 to around AD 380
Arrival of Christianity – around 400
Columbus arrives on Iona – 563
Viking arrivals – around 800
King Kenneth I – 843–859
Donald I – 859–863
Constantine I – 863–877
Aed – 877–878
Eochaig and Giric – 878–889
Donald II – 889–900
Constantine II – 900–943
Malcolm I – 943–954
Indulf – 954–962
Dubh – 962–967
Culen – 967–971
Kenneth II – 971–995
Constantine III – 995–997
Kenneth III – 997–1005
Malcolm II – 1005–1034

Battle of Carham – 1018
Duncan I – 1034–1040
Macbeth – 1040–1057
Lulach – 1057–1058
Malcolm III – 1058–1093
Donald III – 1093–1094
Duncan II – 1094
Donald (again) – 1094–1097
Edgar – 1097–1107
Alexander I – 1107–1124
David I – 1124–1153
Malcolm IV – 1153–1165
William – 1165–1214
Alexander II – 1214–1249
Alexander III – 1249–1286
Battle of Largs – 1263
Margaret – 1286–1290
No monarch – 1290–1292
John Balliol – 1292–1296
No monarch – 1296–1306
Battle of Stirling Bridge – 1297
Robert I (The Bruce) – 1306–1329
Battle of Bannockburn – 1314
Declaration of Arbroath – 1320
David II – 1329–1371
Robert II – 1371–1390
Robert III – 1390–1406
James I – 1406–1437
James II – 1437–1460
James III – 1460–1488

Battle of Sauchieburn – 1488
James IV – 1488–1513
Battle of Flodden – 1513
James V – 1513–1542
Battle of Solway Moss – 1542
Mary I (Queen of Scots) – 1542–1567
James VI (and I) – 1567–1625
Charles I 1625–1649
Charles II – 1649–1685
James VII – 1685–1689
William and – 1689–1702
Mary – 1689–1694
Battle of Killiecrankie – 1689
Glencoe Massacre – 1692
Anne – 1702–1714
Act of Union – 1707
George I – 1714–1727
Jacobite Rebellion – 1715
George II – 1727–1760
Jacobite Rebellion – 1745
George III – 1760–1820
First Spinning Mills – 1779
Comet Steam-ship – 1812
George IV – 1820–1830
William IV – 1830–1837
Railways – from about 1830
Victoria – 1837–1901
Crofters Act – 1886
(Edward VII, George V, Edward VIII, George VI,
    Elizabeth II)

Some Historic Places

Stone Age – Maes Howe and Skara Brae (Orkney)

Stone Circles – Calanais((Lewis), Ring of Brodgar (Orkney)

Brochs – Carloway (Lewis), Glenelg (Highland), Mousa (Shetland)

Crannog – Replica Crannog, Loch Tay

Romans – Antonine Wall remains at Barr Hill, Bearsden, Bonnybridge

Vikings – Remains of settlements, Jarlshof (Shetland), Brough of Birsay (Orkney), Vikingar Exhibition (Largs)

Motte and Bailey – site, Bass of Inverurie

Small Castles – There will be one somewhere near you

Large Castles – Rothesay, Dirleton, Caerlaverock, Bothwell, Threave, Tantallon

Grand Castles – Stirling, Edinburgh, Dumbarton Rock and Castle. Abbeys – and monastic remains – Melrose, Jedburgh, Arbroath

Palaces – Linlithgow, Falkland, Holyrood (Edinburgh)

Tower Houses – Craigievar, Crathes (Aberdeenshire) Claypotts (Broughty Ferry)

Battlefields – Bannockburn, Killiecrankie, Culloden

Grand Houses – Hopetoun House (South Queensferry), House of Dun (Montrose), Pollok House (Glasgow)

Charlotte Square (Edinburgh), Hill House (Helensburgh)

Smaller Houses – Culross, Provost Skene's House (Aberdeen). Gladstone's Land (Edinburgh), The Tenement House (Glasgow), The Black House (Lewis), Auchindrain (Inveraray)